Durham Castle
Fortress, Palace, College

Published by Jeremy Mills Publishing Ltd
for The University College Durham Trust 2007.

www.jeremymillspublishing.co.uk

Text © Richard Brickstock and
The University College Durham Trust 2007.

Images not otherwise attributed are taken almost exclusively
from the University archives or from the author's collection.

ISBN   978-1-905217-24-3

All rights reserved. No part of this book maybe reproduced
in any form, or by any means without prior permission of
the copyright owners.

Every reasonable effort has been made to ensure correct
copyright has been attributed.

Durham Castle
Fortress, Palace, College

Richard Brickstock

Foreword
by Bill Bryson, Chancellor of Durham University

Amble eastward out of central Durham along the tranquil paths that flank the River Wear and in five or six minutes you will come to what I think may be the most pleasing, if not most famous, view in the city.

There, crowning a stately summit above the cheerful jumble of the town below, are the cathedral and castle, both displayed to glorious mutual advantage, particularly on a fine summer's day when their vast surfaces seem not just to reflect the sunlight but somehow to absorb and enrich it before reluctantly letting it go. Here you can see at once why this became one of Britain's first World Heritage Sites – and why it was the whole glorious ensemble and not just the cathedral itself that was selected for designation.

Considering all that it has been in its thousand-year history – fortress, palace, and college – the castle deserves to be better known, and doubtless it would be if it stood on any other hill in England. It is only the soaring, unsurpassable majesty of the cathedral, one of the world's supreme architectural achievements, that gives the castle an air of curious and frankly unwarranted modesty. Anywhere else and it would be a thrusting, rather pugnacious intrusion on the landscape. Here it is a kind of gracious annexe.

The Keep,
Spring 2007.

In fact, as this volume beautifully illustrates, Durham Castle has a history that is as long and as interesting as that of its more famous sister across Palace Green. As the World Heritage citation notes: 'Few buildings in England can boast a longer history of continuous occupation.' Nor, I would venture to add, can there be many with more delightful and little-known treasures within.

The castle contains what is surely the finest room in the north of England in its aptly named Great Hall (which, for the record, stretches 101 feet from end to end and has a ceiling 45 feet high). It has two exquisite chapels, the most imposing, and creakily vertiginous, staircase I know of and some of the most delectable paintings in England.

This is a building, in short, that has long deserved a thorough and engaging written history. And now, I am pleased to say, it has it. So sit back and enjoy the story of what is unquestionably one of the world's most beautiful, fascinating and busily useful of buildings on earth.

Bill Bryson

The Castle from the Cathedral tower.

The University College Durham Trust

by John Hollier

The publication of this book was funded by the University College Durham Trust since it was felt that there would be a strong demand from undergraduates of University College and from the general public for a modern history of the Castle. All profits from the publication will go directly to the Trust and will be used to fund improvements in the amenities available to the undergraduates of University College.

The Trust was set up by former members of University College who were members of the Durham Castlemans Society (now the Durham Castle Society) and is supported by graduates of the College. The primary purpose of the Trust is to fund projects which are for the benefit of the undergraduates of the College. The projects are selected when insufficient funding is available from the University or other sources.

Since the Trust was founded it has contributed to an additional Junior Common Room – the West Courtyard; an extension to the College Library which increased shelf and seating capacity by 50%; and an extension to the West Courtyard JCR. None of these projects would have been possible without the support of the Trust. Currently (in 2006/7) the Trustees have launched a special appeal for money to assist in the restoration of the Tunstal Chapel.

The Castle Keep from the roof of the Great Hall.

Preface
by Richard Brickstock

This is a book about Durham Castle – its buildings, its history and, in particular, its inhabitants. I am conscious of a tremendous debt owed to previous researchers and authors of guides to the history of Durham Castle, but this book will also be something of a personal view of University College since I am not only the Curator of the Durham Castle Museum but also a Castleman (a former student at University College, 1979–83) and a resident of some 25 years standing.

The Castle has had an extremely interesting history, perhaps a curious claim when you consider that it has not been besieged (except by students from Hatfield College!) for some eight and a half centuries. The main interest lies in the range of functions which the buildings have performed: as a fortress; as the principal palace of the Bishops of Durham; and, since 1837, as the home of University College, the foundation college of the University of Durham. The Castle now also houses a Registered Museum, and since 1986 the Cathedral and Castle have been together designated a World Heritage Site.

The following pages will attempt to tell the story of Durham Castle in words and pictures: the opening chapter provides a brief introduction to the Castle in its various guises, and the chapters that follow flesh out the picture of this special building as a stronghold in the North; as the Prince Bishops' residence; as the centre of a thriving College community; and as a Museum open to the general public.

Acknowledgements

I would like to express my gratitude to the many people who have helped to produce this book. Particular thanks are due to the University College Durham Trust (which commissioned the work); my publisher, Jeremy Mills and his staff (for their patience and helpful advice); Duncan Bythell (author of the most recent guidebook, for reading and commenting on the draft text); the late Clive Preece (for commenting on the text, and especially for research on Sanderson Miller and the Maltby china); Ian Doyle (a fount of knowledge on all things relating to the Castle, for allowing me to pick his brains); Kathrin Pieren (for research on conservation); the staff of the Durham University Library, especially Michael Stansfield and Richard Higgins, University College Librarian (for help with the illustrations); Michele Allan and the Design and Imaging Unit, Durham University (for photographic assistance); and, last but not least, my wife Michelle (for her comments and constant encouragement).

The Gatehouse.

Contents

Foreword	*by Bill Bryson*	v
University College Durham Trust	*by John Hollier*	vii
Preface	*by Richard Brickstock*	ix
Acknowledgements		x

Chapter One — 1
Durham Castle, an Introduction

- [1] Durham Castle: fortress, form and function
- [2] Durham Castle: Bishop's Palace
- [3] Durham Castle: University College, University of Durham
- [4] Durham Castle: Museum and World Heritage Site

Chapter Two — 9
Durham Castle as a Fortress

- [1] Early Durham, the Saxon Castle, and the community of St. Cuthbert
- [2] The Norman Castle: the late 11th and 12th centuries
- [3] The Later Middle Ages: the 13th and 14th centuries

Chapter Three — 29
Durham Castle as a Palace

- [1] The 15th century
- [2] The 16th century
- [3] The 17th century
- [4] The 18th and early 19th centuries

Chapter Four — 55
University College and the University of Durham

- [1] Establishing a University
- [2] The first 50 years (1830s–1880s)
- [3] The second 50 years (1880s–1930s)
- [4] The War years (1939–45)
- [5] A time to expand (1945–1980s)
- [6] A mixed and modern college (1987–)

Chapter Five — 91
Durham Castle in the 21st century

- [1] A brief tour of the Castle and College
- [2] Durham Castle Museum
- [3] Caring for a Norman Castle

Chapter Six — 133
The Way Ahead

- [1] Durham Castle and Durham Castle Museum
- [2] Durham Castle and University College
- [3] Durham Castle: Hotel and Conference Centre
- [4] Durham Castle: World Heritage Site

Appendix One	Prince Bishops of Durham	140
Appendix Two	University College Officers	141
Appendix Three	A note on sources	144
Index		146

Chapter One

Durham Castle, An Introduction

[1] Durham Castle: fortress, form and function

Durham Castle stands on the edge of a rocky hill some 35 metres (115 feet) above the River Wear in County Durham about a dozen miles from its estuary at Wearmouth/Sunderland. It blocks off the northern approach to a natural peninsula created by a loop in the river, thereby both dominating its surroundings and affording specific protection to the area, including Durham Cathedral, to the south.

It is likely that a Saxon fortress existed on the site from late in the tenth century, but the earliest parts of the Norman castle were begun in about 1072, some six years after the Conquest, and shortly after the Norman invaders first came to the area. The building was commissioned by King William the Conqueror (1066–87) and carried out under the supervision of Waltheof, Earl of Northumbria, but it was soon handed over by the King to Walcher, Bishop of Durham, and remained in the hands of successive bishops for almost 750 years until the foundation of the University in the 1830s. The Castle thus became the chief residence of the Bishops of Durham who, in addition to their spiritual duties as leaders of the Church, were responsible for the defence and government of the region.

Aerial photograph of the Durham peninsula from the north.

In plan the Castle followed the typical Norman Motte and Bailey form, with a Keep on a mound (or motte) and a walled Courtyard (the Inner Bailey) below it: this layout is still clearly visible despite the many changes that have taken place over the intervening 900 years. Initially the Keep formed a self-contained fortress, probably accessed via a wooden stairway leading to an entrance in the base of its west wall. The Bailey below contained a whole range of buildings, most long gone, though substantial elements of the early Norman castle do survive, incorporated into later buildings, most notably the Norman Chapel, the 11th-century Undercroft below the Great Hall, and the 12th-century Norman range on the north side of the Courtyard.

A dry moat controlled access to the Inner Bailey, which thus had to be approached via a barbican leading to a drawbridge and the Castle's Gatehouse. An Outer Bailey enclosed much of the peninsula, providing walled protection for the monastic community and others, and further fortifications surrounded much of the town to the north. In places the walls of these outer enclosures are still visible, for instance at the Water Gate at the end of the South Bailey, but the majority, including the Great North Gate, the outer gatehouse that guarded the approach up Saddler Street, have since been demolished.

The Norman Arch in the 1840s, by RW Billings.

As a fortress the Castle's function was essentially two-fold: it was a centre from which the population could be controlled, and it provided an obstacle to invasion. In the wake of the Conquest of 1066, the local population was not at first resigned to Norman domination, and the Bishop therefore needed a safe haven for himself and his garrison from which to rule the North on behalf of the King. There was also the apparent threat of further invasion from overseas (a Danish invasion having been defeated at Stamford Bridge by Harold II earlier in 1066), and the very real, and increasing, threat of raids or full-scale invasion from Scotland.

[2] Durham Castle: Bishop's Palace

As well as being a military stronghold, the Castle functioned as the Bishop's ceremonial palace. As the holders of the King's authority in the North, the 'Prince Bishops' were granted extensive powers, such as the right to hold their own courts of law, to raise their own armies and to mint their own coinage. The privileged position of the Prince Bishops and the wealth from their estates meant that Durham Castle could be developed and maintained on a grand scale.

Although the Castle's primary function was initially a military one, the quality of the buildings surviving from Norman times demonstrates the princely lifestyle enjoyed by successive Bishops. The original Great Hall, on the west side of the Courtyard, was soon superseded by grander buildings. It was probably Bishop Flambard (1099–1128) who constructed a new Hall on the north side of the Courtyard, the lower half of which may survive in the present building. However, in the mid-12th century the Castle was badly damaged by fire and Hugh le Puiset (1153–95) rebuilt the west end and upper half of this North Hall.

Durham Castle, An Introduction

The Tunstal Gallery in the 1840s, by Cuthbert Bede.

Despite considerable alterations, the high quality of the workmanship can still be seen in the Norman Arch on the Tunstal Gallery and also along the Norman Gallery.

Modifications to the Castle continued through the Middle Ages, sometimes to improve its military effectiveness but increasingly for the purposes of convenience and/or display. By the early 1300s it had acquired much of its present general appearance. Anthony Bek (1283–1311) was responsible for rebuilding the Great Hall above the old Norman Undercroft on the west side of the Courtyard. Later modifications have covered up most of Bek's work, but some can still be seen in the south-west window of the Hall. Under Thomas Hatfield (1345–81) Bek's Great Hall was extended southwards and the Keep rebuilt in stone. Although the present Keep was reconstructed in 1840 it nonetheless retains Hatfield's octagonal design.

Even less emphasis on defence is evident from the middle of the 15th century, with virtually all subsequent additions to the Castle being made to increase the comfort of residents or to impress visitors. Richard Fox (1494–1501) converted Hatfield's extension to the Great Hall into apartments and the south-west tower into the present Kitchen. A generation later Cuthbert Tunstal (1530–59) was responsible for major additions to the Castle along the north side of the Courtyard – a new Chapel and its attendant stair-turret as well as the two-storey Gallery that leads from the Great Hall to the Chapel.

The bishopric was abolished by Parliament in 1646 during the English Civil War and the Castle sold, but after the Restoration of the Monarchy in 1660 the building was repaired and modernised by subsequent Bishops. A huge amount of work was undertaken by John Cosin (1660–72), his most spectacular addition being the great staircase in the north-west corner of the Courtyard, known (from its woodwork) as the Black Stairs.

Cosin was the last Bishop of Durham to make major additions to the structure of the Castle, although later Bishops, notably Nathaniel Lord Crewe (1674–1721), Joseph Butler (1750–52) and Richard Trevor (1752–71) continued to make alterations and additions to suit their own tastes, until finally the Castle was handed over to the University in the 1830s.

The Black Stairs.

[3] Durham Castle: University College, University of Durham

Today Durham Castle is occupied by University College, the foundation college of the University of Durham. The University was founded in 1832 by Bishop Van Mildert (1826–36) and the Dean and Chapter of the Cathedral. Ambitious plans were drawn up for a large complex of college buildings on the west side of Palace Green, between the Cathedral and the Castle – but came to nothing. Instead, existing buildings were adapted for University use: in particular, after Van Mildert's death the Castle was handed over to the University, and became the home of University College.

There was, however, a lack of rooms suitable for student accommodation, and the first students appear to have lived in rather dilapidated rooms in University House, now known as Cosin's Hall, on the east side of Palace Green. The reconstruction in 1840 of the Castle's Keep provided more sought-after accommodation, and the rooms off the Norman Gallery were also converted to provide student rooms (and are even now occupied in term by student officers of the College).

Student numbers remained modest during the College's first century of existence, and even during the 1930s there were often fewer than 40 students in residence. After the Second World War, however, numbers expanded rapidly, so that by the early 1950s the College had over 200 undergraduate and postgraduate students. During the 50s and 60s the numbers continued to rise, and University College students occupied Lumley Castle (about 8 miles away, near Chester-le-Street) as well as Durham for some 23 years before the opening of purpose-built accommodation in Bailey Court (1970) and Moatside Court (1977). The College's newest building (1991) is a new office and accommodation block in the Fellows' Garden.

Recently the number of students attending the University as a whole has again greatly increased, and University College has likewise expanded. The College admitted women for the first time in 1987, at which time the Castle had some 330 students in total. A further rapid expansion brought the number up to about 480 in 1992, by which stage numbers had outstripped the available accommodation so that the majority of undergraduates (previously housed by the College for their entire student career) had to 'live out' in their second year at Durham.

The number of undergraduate and postgraduate members of University College passed 650 with the beginning of the new millennium and is now well past the 700 mark. Of these, rather more than half live 'in College', though only about 80 of them in the Castle itself, for the majority of students at University College now live outside the Castle in purpose-built student accommodation and rented houses.

A Norman Gallery sitting room in the 1840s, by Cuthbert Bede.

The Castle still provides the College's Dining Hall, Common Rooms (including a thriving Senior Common Room which has several hundred members), Chapels, Library and Bar, and many social and official functions of the University are held in the Great Hall and State Rooms. In addition, particularly during the vacations when the undergraduates are not in residence, the Castle takes on yet more roles, as a conference centre, as an hotel and as the setting for numerous wedding receptions.

[4] Durham Castle: Museum and World Heritage Site

Since 1989 the collections at Durham Castle have constituted a formally registered museum (holding Provisional Registration until the achievement of Full Registration in 2002), a status that indicates that the Durham Castle Museum reaches nationally approved standards of recording and care for its collections. Since 1998 the College has employed a part-time Curator; prior to that care for the collections was undertaken by amateurs working within the formal framework of the Historic Buildings and Contents sub-committee of the College's Governing Body.

The Castle Museum is unusual in a number of respects, not least in that it is contained within a living and working college community: the collections are scattered around the College and University, largely, but by no means exclusively, within the Great Hall and State Rooms of the Castle, and many of the objects are in regular, if not daily, use. Thus, although the Castle has been open to the public for many years, admission has to be by guided tour only, so as not to conflict with the day-to-day running of the College. Even so, the Castle receives something of the order of 35–40,000 visitors each year.

Formal dinner in the Great Hall, c.1960.

The Great Hall, built by Bishop Bek (1283–1311); later modifications include the porch and oriental-style buttresses of Bishop Cosin (1660–72).

The Castle is also unusual in that it has never been a family seat – the Bishopric was not hereditary – and the building therefore differs in significant ways from the 'average' stately home. This in turn affects both the character of the Castle and the makeup of the Museum's collections, for each new Bishop had to bring his own furnishings (and remove them when he left). Many Bishops looked to leave their mark by adding to or altering the buildings themselves, adapting them to new (and sometimes short-lived) uses – and this is reflected in the wide range of architectural styles visible within the Castle.

In 1986 Durham Castle and Durham Cathedral were jointly designated by UNESCO as a World Heritage Site, one of the first series of British sites to be so designated. This is a very prestigious award, but one which, unfortunately, has not yet yielded the benefits (financial or otherwise) which one might reasonably expect to accrue from such an exalted status.

At the time of writing, the University is in need of something of the order of £8 million to undertake increasingly urgent restoration of the stonework and general fabric of Durham Castle. However, it is often hard to satisfy the funding criteria of the various bodies (such as the Heritage Lottery Fund) which might provide financial support, partly because the building houses an educational institution.

In 1999 the Castle was therefore placed on English Heritage's 'Buildings at risk' register and categorized, on a scale of A–F, as Grade C, 'suffering slow decay; no solution agreed'. Rather than to castigate the University authorities for their failure to look after the building, this move was intended by English Heritage to highlight the plight of the building and perhaps make it easier for the University to obtain financial aid towards its restoration.

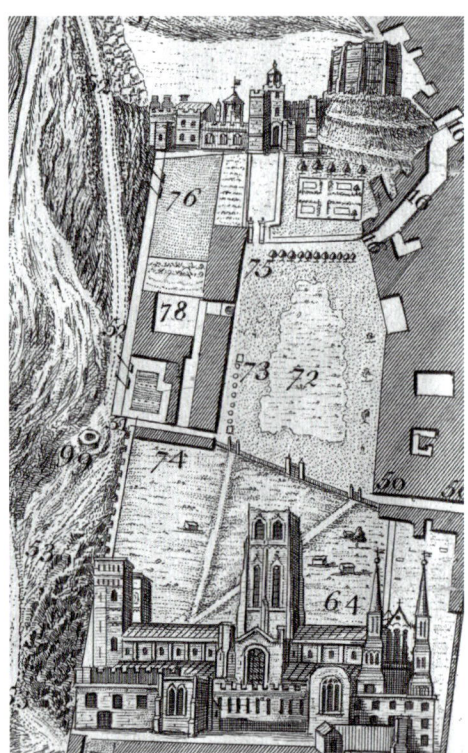

The Castle, Cathedral and Palace Green; a detail taken from Forster's map of 1754.

The Castle and Cathedral from the railway station.

Chapter Two

Durham Castle as a Fortress

[1] Early Durham, the Saxon Castle and the Community of St. Cuthbert

After the end of the last Ice Age, some 10,000 years ago, nomadic Stone Age peoples gradually re-colonized what is now north-east England, and their Neolithic and Bronze Age successors established a number of small settlements in the region between *c.*3000 and 700 BC. Evidence for pre-Roman occupation of the Durham peninsula itself is, however, very slight. Iron Age occupation (after *c.*700 BC) in the immediate vicinity seems to have centred on the hill-top site at Maiden Castle, a mile upstream from the modern city centre: although the River Wear has since moved away across its floodplain, in the Iron Age its precipitous river cliffs provided a more suitable site for a hill-fort there – and, as a result, the area on which the modern city is centred seems to have been largely overlooked.

In the Roman period, Julius Caesar led two expeditions across what we now know as the English Channel in the 50s BC, but it was not until AD 43, in the reign of the Emperor Claudius, that the Romans began in earnest their attempted conquest of Britain, and a further three decades before they advanced as far north as modern-day Yorkshire and Co. Durham. Thus it was not until the early 70s that the North-East saw Roman legions for the first time, when the Emperor Vespasian ordered the annexation of the territory of the tribe of the Brigantes (a vast tract of land spanning both sides of the Pennines and extending from Humberside up into what is now southern Scotland).

Even then the site now occupied by Durham seems to have been largely ignored. The Romans, on the attack, were more interested in protecting sites of strategic importance than in providing defensible fortresses for their troops. Their forts were therefore built down on the river floodplains, guarding important crossing points, rather than on neighbouring hilltops, and civil settlements (*vici*) grew up around the forts. In this region, the most important Roman road, Dere Street, passed well to the west of where Durham now stands, and the most important sites were established where the various roads bridged or forded rivers – at Piercebridge on the Tees; Binchester and Chester-le-Street, in the Wear valley, respectively south and north of modern Durham; and, to the north-west, Lanchester on the Browney and Ebchester on the Derwent.

The Castle from the west.

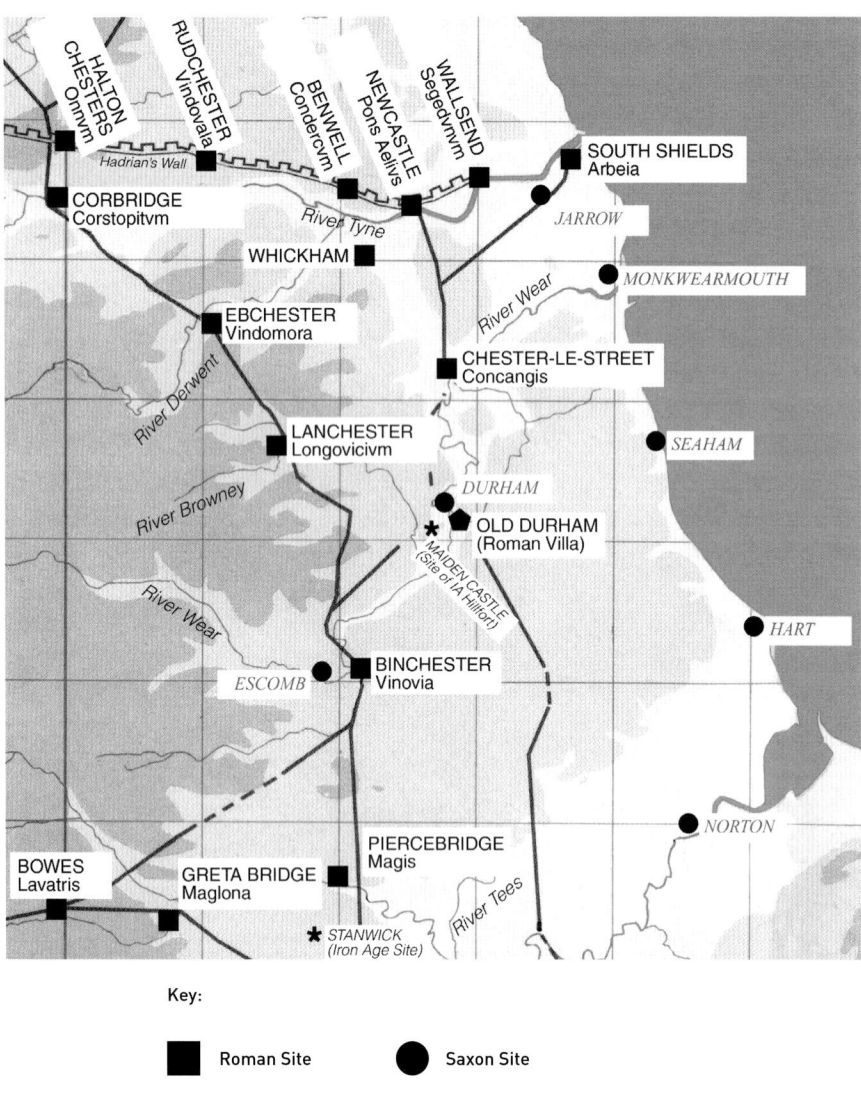

Regional map showing principal Iron Age, Roman and Saxon sites.

There was certainly some Roman activity closer to Durham: at Old Durham (a hamlet just across the river from Maiden Castle), a small baths-block, discovered in the 1940s, suggests the existence of a Roman *villa*, a well-appointed, Romanised farm, perhaps taking the place of an earlier native farmstead. However, the Roman finds from the Durham peninsula itself, isolated pot-sherds or individual coins, can almost be counted on the fingers of one hand, and nothing definite is known of any settlement there.

With the passing of Roman domination, in the early 5th century, local rulers and populations appear to have relied initially on the stone walls of the old Roman settlements such as Chester-le-Street on the Wear and South Shields on the Tyne. Eventually, however, the Saxon communities began to construct their own towns and fortifications in more obviously-defensible positions – and the history of Durham proper begins with this change of outlook.

The first literary mention of Durham may be in the *Anglo-Saxon Chronicle*, which recorded the consecration of one Peohtwine as Bishop of Whithorn in 762 at *Aelfet ee*, Aelfet Island: it is possible this was Elvet, on Durham's eastern margin. There is, however, no direct archaeological evidence for Saxon settlement anywhere on or around the peninsula at this early date.

Nevertheless, a Saxon fortress probably existed on the Durham peninsula from late in the 10th century (if not earlier): archaeological evidence certainly seems to suggest that the Saxon Earl Uchtred had established a defended fortress town (a *burg*) here by that time, and the present castle may occupy the site of the Earl's fortifications. The form of these defences is unknown, but the most essential element would have been a barrier across the neck of the peninsula, controlling access from the north – perhaps a wall, but more likely an earthen bank topped by a palisade and fronted by a ditch, defences very similar, therefore, to those of the earlier hillfort at nearby Maiden Castle. The castle mound, almost certainly an artificial one, may also have been constructed at this time.

In AD 995 the monks of St. Cuthbert (the North-East's pre-eminent saint) found their way to Dunholme, or Durham, from their previous resting place at Chester-le-Street – and from this time onwards there was therefore an additional reason for the region's rulers to fortify and defend the Durham peninsula, namely to provide protection for the growing cult of the saint.

The monks were the successors of a community founded by St. Aidan on Lindisfarne (Holy Island) in the 630s. On Holy Island, although close to the Northumbrian royal castle at Bamburgh, they were vulnerable to seaborne raids and suffered badly in the first Viking attack of 793. In 875, after enduring a further series of raids, the monks finally decided to leave Lindisfarne. They took with them the wooden church built by St. Aidan as well as the relics of their most famous saints, including the body and coffin of St. Cuthbert. In 883, after eight years of wandering that included a stay at Norham, the community eventually found a new home at the old Roman station at Chester-le-Street on the banks of the River Wear, and stayed there for over a century.

Little is known of Chester-le-Street at that period, but it is likely that it was inhabited throughout the post-Roman and Anglo-Saxon periods and that the monks therefore found the site already partially occupied. Roman stonework probably remained sufficiently intact to afford the community some protection, and perhaps also to provide some accommodation for the new arrivals. Recent excavations, undertaken when the modern car park adjacent to the ancient parish

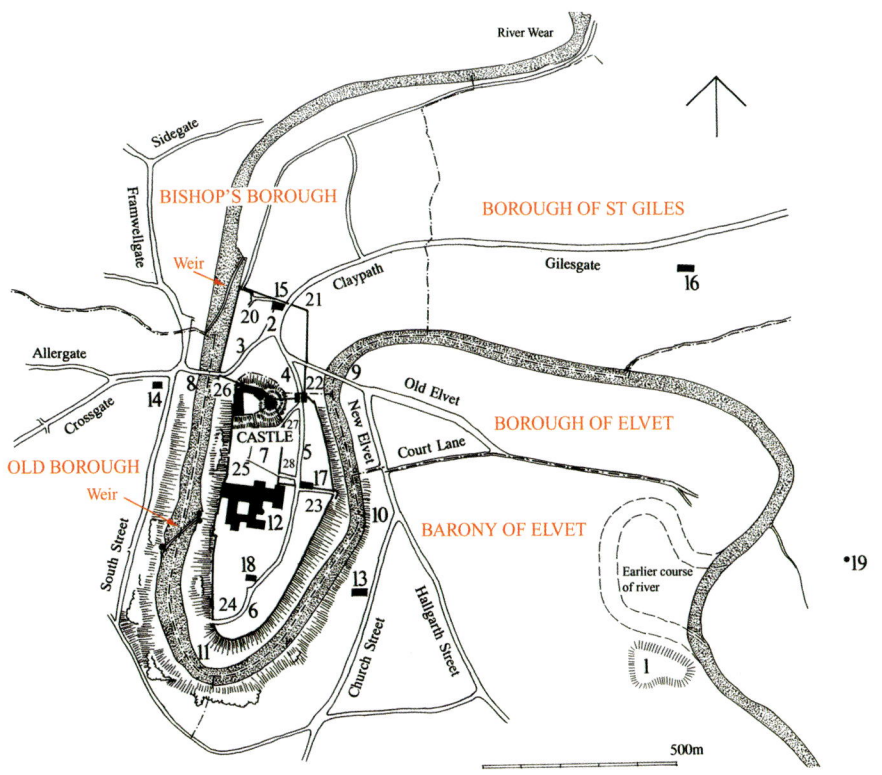

Saxon and early Medieval Durham (after Roberts, 2003).

1	Maiden Castle (Site of IA Hillfort)		CHURCHES
		12	Cathedral and Priory
		13	St Oswald
		14	St Margaret
		15	St Nicholas
STREETS		16	St Giles
2	Market Place	17	St Mary-le-Bow
3	Silver Street	18	St Mary-the-Less
4	Saddler Street	19	Old Durham Roman Villa (site of)
5	North Bailey		
6	South Bailey		
7	Palace Green		GATES
BRIDGES		20	Walkergate
8	Framwellgate Bridge (c.1120)	21	Clayport
		22	North Gate
9	Elvet Bridge (later C12th)	23	Kingsgate
		24	Watergate
10	Bow Bridge (site of)	25	Postern Gate
11	Ford (site of) superseded in 1574 by Prebends Bridge	26	Framwellgate
		27	Owengate
		28	Lyegate

church was extended, revealed the remains of Roman barrack blocks, thus indicating that the 11th-century church occupies a fairly central position within the earlier Roman fortress. This church may itself overlie an earlier church erected by the monastic community (conceivably the wooden church of St. Aidan that they certainly carried with them as far as Norham).

Chester-le-Street, however, although it once had a curtain wall, had never been heavily defended, even in the Roman period, and was not in a readily-defensible position – and it may be for this reason that the monks eventually abandoned the town and, in 995, moved about eight miles south to Durham (via a brief stay in Ripon), looking once more for protection against raiding by the Danes and now also by the Scots.

The monastic community was led by Bishop Aldhun of Chester-le-Street, father-in-law of Uchtred, Earl of Northumbria. The move to Durham no doubt suited both Bishop and Earl: Aldhun and his community gained the Earl's protection, while Uchtred enjoyed his close association with the growing fame of the cult of St. Cuthbert. The community had once again transported its relics, and these were housed first in a temporary shelter, then in a wooden church (the White Church), and finally in a great stone church, founded in 998 and built using local labour provided by the Earl. The remains of this new church are hidden beneath the precincts of the Norman cathedral just as the Norman castle complex hides any predecessor of its own.

It seems more than likely that a Saxon fortress of some kind was already in existence at the turn of the first millennium when the Community of St. Cuthbert arrived, but if this was not the case, fortifications must then have been rapidly constructed, for it is known that the city was successfully defended against Scottish attack in 1006 and again in 1040. Unfortunately, the existence and shape of the Saxon castle and/or fortifications are almost entirely conjectural, since whatever evidence there may be underlies the present buildings and therefore cannot readily be recovered.

Evidence for the Saxon town is much stronger, indicating a number of small communities on and around the peninsula, huddling under the protection of the conjectured fortifications. The archaeological evidence for the period derives partly from excavations in the 1970s, led by Prof. Martin Carver, which preceded the building of University College's student accommodation in Moatside Court off Saddler Street, the approach road leading up to the Castle gateway. Those excavations revealed the remains of wattle and daub houses, of the tenth century or earlier, just outside the curtain wall of the Norman Castle, as well as the extensive remains of shoe making and other leatherwork (appropriately enough, given the later name of the road).

[2] The Norman Castle: the late 11th and 12th centuries

Today the skyline of Durham is dominated not by the Saxon buildings but by the great Norman Cathedral and, to a lesser extent, the Castle: the view from the railway viaduct is justly famous as one of the great sights of the North – and in earlier times, when the city was smaller and other buildings were not so tall, that dominance must have been even more obvious. The Castle, although often overshadowed by the Cathedral complex, is particularly impressive from the north (for example as you approach down the modern A690, the Sunderland Road).

The Castle in the mid-1970s with, on the right, Moatside Court under construction.

Durham Castle: Fortress, Palace, College

In 1066 the peace of Saxon England was shattered by the invasions of the Danes under Harald Hardrada and the Normans led by Duke William. King Harold II came north and defeated the Danes at Stamford Bridge near York, but then fell in the subsequent battle at Hastings against William. The new King, William (the Conqueror), took some time to establish his rule, particularly in the North, and Durham was to feature strongly in the process.

Initially William delegated control of the north of the kingdom to his Earl of Northumbria. In less than three years, however, two Earls had been murdered and a third had rebelled. The King's answer was to send north an army of 700 men led by a new Earl, Robert Cumin. The potential importance of Durham appears already to have been appreciated at this stage, but it was clearly less than impregnable as a fortress: Cumin entered Durham with his soldiers on 30 January 1069, only to meet his death the very next day when the local populace invaded the peninsula, set fire to his house and slaughtered his army.

The Conqueror's response was the 'Harrying of the North': he came north himself with another army, devastating much of the countryside between York and Durham, though Durham itself was spared. William therefore passed through the city in

The Castle, from the north, still dominates the town.

1069, but the Norman Castle does not appear to have been begun until after his return from Scotland in 1072:

'At the same time as the King was turned back from Scotland he founded a castle in Durham, where the bishop and his men could be safe from raids...' (Extract from the *History of the Kings*, attributed to Simeon, monk of Durham).

Work on the Castle began under the supervision of Waltheof, Earl of Northumbria, and was continued, after the Earl's murder in 1075, by Walcher, Bishop of Durham (1071–80), in whose hands the Bishopric and Earldom were first combined. The Castle thus became the chief residence of the Bishop of Durham, from which he ruled a large swathe of the North in the King's name, and it remained almost continuously in the hands of successive bishops for 750 years.

The Norman Castle was built with clear military objectives in mind: the conquering Normans were relatively few in number, and the local population was far from pacified, so the new rulers needed strongly-defended safe havens, such as the Durham peninsula, from which to continue their operations. In addition, it needed to guard against any further threat from overseas (for the Danish threat had not entirely evaporated with their defeat in 1066) and to provide protection against raids or full-scale invasion from Scotland.

Durham Castle was therefore intended both to dominate the surrounding area and to throw a strong defensive screen across the narrow neck of the peninsula, at that point only a few hundred yards across (for the river comes in from the north-east, swings around the city in a great loop, and then flows away northwards towards Chester-le-Street and the sea at Wearmouth, in modern-day Sunderland). The Castle occupied a commanding position on the main road south, so that potential invaders from the north would have to take the Castle before advancing, or risk being threatened from behind – but the Norman fortifications, greatly aided by rock foundations and steep river cliffs, made the peninsula virtually impregnable.

Under the Normans, therefore, Durham rapidly became a more useful fortress. An expected attack by the Danes in 1075 did not materialise, so the new defences went untested, but only five years later, when Bishop Walcher was murdered by a mob at Gateshead, his retainers fled to the Castle, and its fortifications were by then clearly strong enough for them to hold out against the local population until help could arrive. William was provoked by this act of rebellion into sending yet another army – and from its garrison base in Durham it once again laid waste much of the area in reprisal for the opposition to Norman rule.

The growing power of the fortress was further demonstrated under the next Bishop, William de St. Calais (1080–96), who in 1088 joined a rebellion of Norman barons against the new King, William Rufus (1087–1100). The rebellion was soon repressed, but the Bishop was safe from arrest within the walls of his Castle. He was eventually persuaded to attend trial in London and was sent into exile, but after three years he was allowed to return to Durham and in 1093 he began work on the great Norman Cathedral. The Cathedral was sited on the peninsula, south of the Castle and therefore enjoying its protection, and further south yet were the buildings of the newly-founded Benedictine priory which took over guardianship of the relics of St. Cuthbert.

Bishop Rannulph Flambard (1099–1128) strengthened the city still further, building a stronger and higher wall of stone around the peninsula, enclosing what was in effect the Castle's Outer Bailey and replacing what might up to then have been only an earthen rampart.

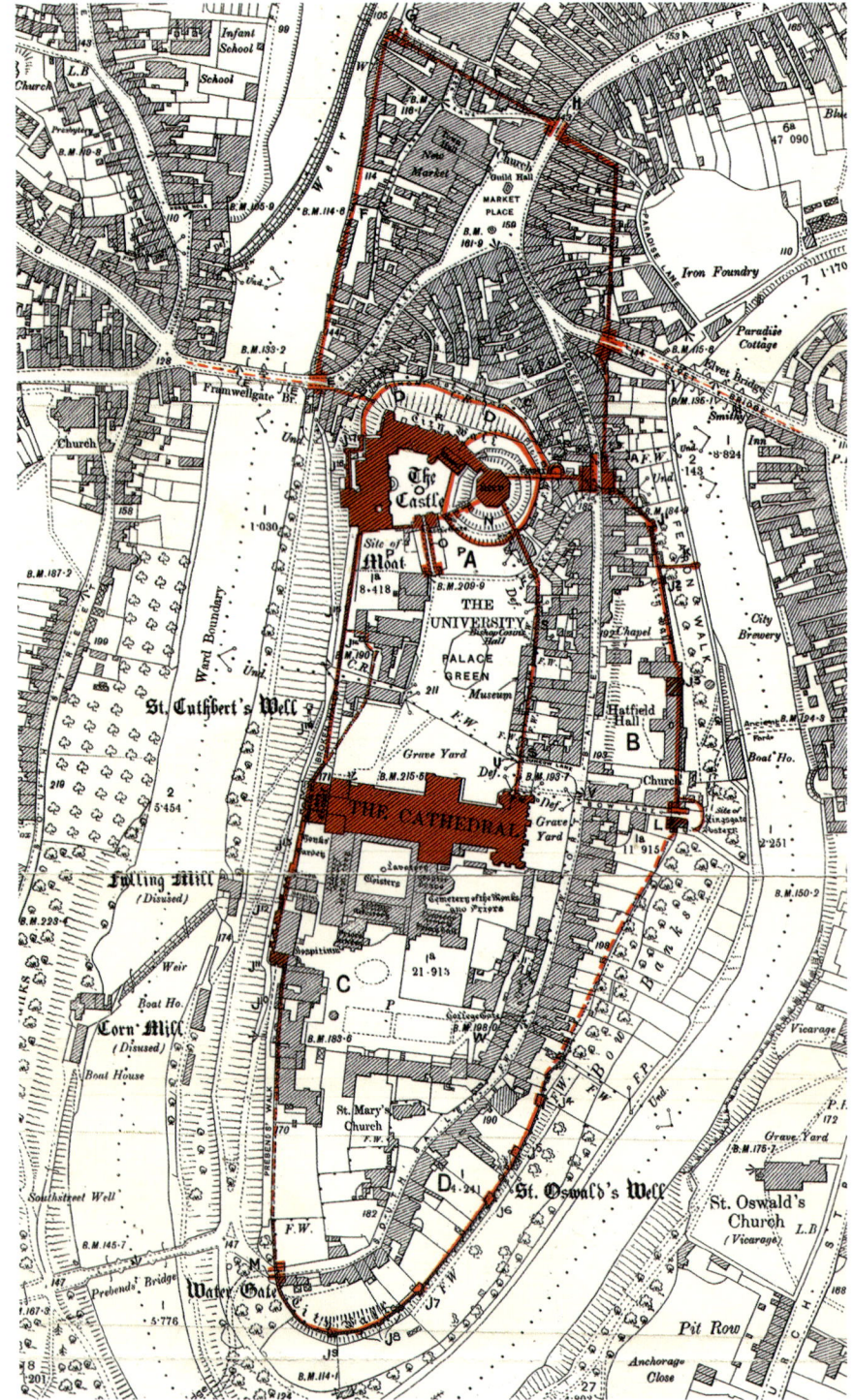

Map of the Durham peninsula with the defences shown in red (published in the Durham University journal, April 1921).

He also divided the Bailey by building a wall between the east end of the Cathedral and the Castle's Keep, cleared many of the dwellings between the Castle and the Cathedral to create the open area now known as Palace Green, and excavated the dry moat around the Castle itself. The Motte and the Inner Bailey of the Castle were already in existence at this date, the former a mound some forty-five feet high topped by a timber Keep, and it was probably Flambard who constructed a stone wall to surround the Keep, perhaps replacing an earlier timber palisade.

By this time the Bishop was effectively a 'Prince-Bishop', and within the Palatinate of Durham he enjoyed privileges which elsewhere belonged only to the King. His lands also included North Durham, an area south of the Tweed, on the border with Scotland – and there, at Norham, Flambard in 1121 built another motte-and-bailey Castle.

At this stage, Durham Castle's primary function was still military, though it is clear that considerable attention was already being given to the internal arrangements. Inside the Inner Bailey, to the west of the Keep, various ranges of rooms already existed by Flambard's time – on the west, north, east and perhaps also the south sides of the Courtyard – but our knowledge of them is imperfect.

On the west side was the Great (West) Hall, built in the late 11th century, almost certainly by Bishop Walcher: little is known about it, for although its Undercroft survives, the Hall was demolished in the late 13th century to make way for its successor.

On the north side of the Courtyard, behind the curtain wall defences was the 'Norman Chapel', probably part of a more extensive range of rooms which do not now survive. Although now dedicated as a chapel, its original function is not certain. It was probably a chapel from the start, but there are two other possibilities: it may have been, as it seems to have become, the crypt to a chapel above it (for it is thought that there was a chapel in that position between the 12th and 16th centuries, where the Senate Room now stands); or (perhaps the least likely option) it may even have been a secular building, perhaps the undercroft of a small hall.

It is just conceivable that this part of the Castle is a survival from an earlier building, a late Saxon Palace built by Earl Uchtred or his successors. If it was a Saxon Hall, however, the Normans changed its function, for Prior Laurence of Durham, writing in the 1140s, mentions it (or perhaps the building above it):

'There is also a shining chapel here supported upon six columns not too large, but quite lovely.'

The Norman Chapel, complete with early capitals and, on the right of the picture, an alcove thought by some to have been a sally port in the northern defences.

A mid-9th century pre-Romanesque palace in Asturias, now the church of Santa María del Naranco, provides a possible continental parallel. Close affinities to the shape of the Norman Chapel may also be seen in Normandy and other parts of northern France in buildings of the second half of the 11th century.

The capitals in the Norman Chapel are conspicuously lacking in overt Christian symbolism; these examples show a stag hunt and a snake.

It is much more likely, however, that the 'Norman Chapel' is a very early part of the Norman Castle, constructed against the newly-built curtain wall by Bishop Walcher (between 1072 and about 1080) or by his immediate successor, Bishop St. Calais (in the 1080s).

Whatever its date and purpose, it is a most astonishing survival. Built at Courtyard level, it was well-lit by three large windows in its east wall (unfortunately blocked by the extension of the mound in the mid-14th century) and it retains much of its original herring-bone pattern floor. Its chief glory, however, lies in its veined sandstone columns, each topped by intricately-carved capitals.

An East Range was probably also built by Walcher, for limited excavations in the 1990s revealed herring-bone flooring (a close match for that of the Chapel) and pieces of painted wall plaster, the remains, it seems, of several high-status rooms dating to the late-11th century or thereabouts. This range, however, seems to have survived only a few years before being removed by Flambard.

Another building, a two-storey accommodation block of rather lesser quality, was built against the south wall of the Chapel, probably by St. Calais. This, again, does not survive, though the garderobe (toilet block) that ran south from it towards the East Range still exists (and is accessible via a manhole cover in the Courtyard). A stairway from the upper floor gave access to the Norman Chapel (the ground-floor entrance to which may have been blocked by the new building).

On the south side of the Courtyard, towards the western corner, was the original Gatehouse, the entranceway to the

Inner Bailey. Flambard rebuilt the Gatehouse further east (perhaps explaining the destruction of the East Range, which would then have obstructed access to the Courtyard). Stonework from the original Gatehouse and other conjectured buildings in the south-west corner of the Courtyard appears to have been incorporated into the lower levels of later buildings, namely the Garden Stairs block and the Kitchens.

Flambard was also responsible for the construction of a large and imposing North Hall between the Chapel and the north end of the West Hall, and from this time on the Castle could boast two great Halls, a circumstance that seems to have impressed Prior Laurence:

'It [the Inner Bailey] *displays two great palaces embellished with porticos....*', presumably a reference to Walcher's West and Flambard's North Halls.

To make room for the North Hall, the west end of the almost-new accommodation block and the stairway to the ground-floor Chapel must have been swept away. The Hall was built at first-floor level over a series of now-blind arcades (the latter perhaps concealing the remains of the Saxon defences). It seems logical that the Chapel was also relocated at first-floor level at this time (assuming it was not already there). Spiral staircases at either end of the new range gave access to the Hall (and thereafter, until the 1840s, to what is now known as the 'Norman Chapel').

The importance of Durham in guarding the northern marches was once more apparent in the period after the death of Henry I (1100–35), when a civil war ensued between his nephew King Stephen (1135–54) and his daughter, the Empress Matilda. David I of Scotland invaded the north in 1136 in support of Matilda and threatened Durham, but was halted by Stephen, who then occupied the city. Two years later a further Scottish invasion was heavily defeated near Northallerton at the Battle of the Standard, and David was forced to sue for peace. Nonetheless, in the treaty of Durham signed in 1139, Stephen granted David extremely favourable terms, including the Earldom of Northumberland – and the Bishopric became for a time 'an oasis in a Scottish Northumbria'.

On the death of Bishop Geoffrey Rufus (1133–40), the Scottish Chancellor, William Cumin, usurped the Bishopric and seized the Castle. Although the Castle subsequently changed hands on several occasions, this could perhaps be described as the last successful 'siege'. Because of the strength of the Castle, Cumin was able to defy all comers until eventually forced to resign the see in favour of the legitimate appointee, William of St. Barbara (1143–1152).

The next Bishop, Hugh le Puiset (or Pudsey; 1153–95), nephew of King Stephen, inherited a fairly parlous situation – Cumin had devastated much of the area, and the Bishop's lands were surrounded by Scottish territory – but under him Durham enjoyed a period of stability and its power and fortunes saw a dramatic up-turn. As Scottish influence waned le Puiset re-established the Bishop's role as the King's regent in the North; he rebuilt the suburbs of Elvet and St.Giles; he built Elvet Bridge, linking Elvet and the city; he granted the first charter to the Bishop's Borough, north of the town (in 1179); he completed the Galilee Chapel at the Cathedral; – and he built extensively within the Castle. By the end of his 42 years as Bishop, therefore, Durham had become a major centre of pilgrimage; a prosperous small town; and the centre of power in the North.

In the early years of his episcopate, however, there was a serious fire in Durham which destroyed much of the town and badly damaged the Castle. Le Puiset restored the fire-damaged buildings, in particular Flambard's north range, probably creating a pair of Halls, one above the other, with various state apartments at either end.

Part of the Upper Hall survives as the Norman Gallery, but most of the interior of the Lower Hall has vanished beneath later remodelling. In truth, the precise layout of le Puiset's building is hard to reconstruct: it is possible that the centre of the block was originally a single Hall reaching to the rafters, though perhaps with a gallery running around the walls at the present Norman Gallery level – but it is more likely that there were two floor levels from the start. If so, the Upper Hall was probably the Bishop's main audience chamber, in which case the Lower Hall would have been the Constable's Hall, housing both that official (who ran the Castle on behalf of the Bishop) and the Bishop's militia.

The ornate entranceway to the range, now known as the Norman Arch, is at first-floor level and was once approached via a flight of stairs from the Courtyard. The doorway, a fabulous example of mid-12th century stone carving, is particularly well-preserved, suggesting that the stairway was protected by a canopy.

The footings of the Norman Arch suggest that the level of the Lower Hall was perhaps a foot or two lower than the present (18th-century) floor level in the Senior Common Room, though the east end was raised somewhat: the short flight of stairs immediately east of the Arch led to a 'solar' where the Senate Lobby now stands. Thus the Lower Hall, though at first-floor level relative to the Courtyard, was at ground-floor level relative to the northern side of the Castle. The lowest apartments were probably at a slightly lower level (corresponding to the anteroom to

The Norman Arch shown on an early 20th-century postcard.

The Upper Hall (now the Norman Gallery) by Nichols and Sons, 1838, showing the carved Romanesque windows (and window-seats) as well as the main doorway at the head of the spiral staircase.

the present Senior Common Room and the Judges' Kitchen), with a second layer above (corresponding to the present Bishop's Suite at the west end, on the same level as the 'solar').

Windows on the northern side, if they existed at all, were probably small (at this lower level), for the north wall was an important part of the defensive screen surrounding the Inner Bailey. Sufficient light may well have been provided by larger windows in the south wall of the range, but the surviving windows (now hidden behind the lath and plaster walls of the Senior Common Room) are much later, probably 15th-century.

An additional spiral stair to the east of the Norman Arch gave access to the Upper Hall, and the two spirals at either end of the range allowed communication between the various apartments. Originally, this Upper Hall would have been twice the height and width of the current Norman Gallery, for both the ceiling and the rooms on the north side are later additions. However, substantial amounts of le Puiset's decorative stonework survive along the south and west walls of the Gallery (work that was matched on the north side, at this higher and less vulnerable level), allowing some appreciation of the grandeur of Hall as it was first conceived.

[3] The Later Middle Ages: the 13th and 14th centuries

In the centuries that followed the Castle for the most part enjoyed a rather quieter history. As the area became accustomed to Norman rule, the Bishop had less need of the Castle as a refuge from his subjects, but it had, by then, become a powerful political symbol and it continued to fulfil its other roles, protecting the city and the Cathedral from attack and, through its sheer impregnability, deterring foreign invasion of the North.

The 'Prince Bishop', or 'Count Palatine', as the Bishop of Durham is frequently termed, ruled the 'Palatinate' (the 'County Palatine'; modern County Durham and more besides) as the King's deputy in the North. As such he enjoyed extensive powers and privileges including the right to raise his own armies, to hold his own courts of law and to mint his own coinage.

Under Anthony Bek (1283–1311), variously styled Prince Palatine, Lord of the Isle of Man and Patriarch of Jerusalem, the Bishop's power and importance increased yet further, partly because of the prominence of the North in the events of the period. The Scottish King, John Balliol, had been appointed by Edward I of England, at the Scots' request, from amongst several rival candidates for the throne – and Balliol had acknowledged Edward as his overlord. In 1296, however, Balliol refused to attend Edward's parliament in Newcastle, Edward invaded Scotland in reprisal, and the Bishop of Durham went with him, leading an army of 26 standard-bearers, 140 knights, 500 cavalry and 1000 foot-soldiers. This was no token involvement of the Bishop in the political and military arena, for in 1298 Bek was in command of one wing of the English army which defeated William Wallace at Falkirk.

The Bishop did not always have things entirely his own way, however, for the Bishop of Durham was, within the church hierarchy, subordinate to the Archbishop of York and thus liable to some interference from that quarter. In addition, and closer to home, the Cathedral Priory of Durham exercised a considerable degree of independence which at times brought it into conflict with the Bishop – and this in spite of the fact that the Priory's lands and privileges derived from the Bishop. These were, however, relatively minor thorns in the side of successive Bishops, who were, so long as they did not incur the King's displeasure, the undisputed rulers of the region.

The Bishop's temporal power was emphasised by the fact that neither the County nor the City of Durham were represented in Parliament by knights or burgesses – a situation that pertained until as late as 1674. Legal cases within the Palatinate were decided in the Bishop's own courts, and the Bishop appointed his own Chancellor to oversee them. Various cases could be referred to the Crown, or carried a right of appeal to the Crown, but even so, through the existence of these courts, considerable power was concentrated in the hands of the Bishop – and the Chancery Court of the County Palatine was to survive, albeit in much altered form, right up to 1975.

The Bishop also enjoyed a substantial income, much of it derived from the people over whom he ruled – and we have quite a detailed knowledge of this thanks to Hugh le Puiset who, in the 1180s, commissioned an assessment of his estate – the 'Boldon Book' as it is now known – listing the rents and labour due to the Bishop as overlord. In addition to the profits from farming the land, the Bishop was also allowed to exploit the other natural resources of the region – iron, coal, timber, and so on. Particularly important was the right, granted by King Stephen to le Puiset, to mine lead, and also to retain any silver extracted from the ore: the percentage of silver in Weardale lead ore was always low, but it was nonetheless a profitable by-product.

A silver penny of the Durham mint. Durham mint coins can typically be distinguished by the stamp of a bishop's mitre and/or the initials of the bishop – in this example TW for Thomas Wolsey.

The privilege of minting silver coinage on behalf of the crown, albeit only the lower denominations, was another major source of revenue for successive Bishops, though it was by no means a privilege to be relied upon: in 1157, in le Puiset's time, King Henry II established a mint at Newcastle after the town's surrender by Malcolm of Scotland – and the Boldon Book makes it clear that the operation of that mint drastically reduced the revenue of the bishop's dies, from ten to three marks per annum. Eventually, the King actually removed the dies from the Bishop, thus revoking his privilege – but they were restored to the next Bishop, Philip of Poitou, consecrated in 1197.

The mint continued in (slightly intermittent) activity until closed for good in 1535 along with the other ecclesiastical mints (Canterbury, York, etc.) after Henry VIII's break with Rome. The last two Bishops of Durham to enjoy the privilege were Thomas Wolsey (1523–29), whose coins bear his initials, T W; and Cuthbert Tunstal (1530–59), whose coins are marked C D, Cuthbert Dunelm (i.e. Durham). Wolsey was simultaneously both Bishop of Durham and Archbishop of York – but although he enjoyed the revenues of Durham, he never deigned to appear in the Palatinate; on his fall from royal favour, one of the charges laid against him was that he had exceeded his powers as Archbishop by causing his initials to be stamped not only on silver pennies but also on groats (4d pieces). A fair proportion of the Bishops' income was spent on the Castle, to make it both a more effective fortress and a more imposing residence – and the late 13th and 14th centuries saw another great period of building activity at Durham Castle.

As well as being a great soldier and politician, Bishop Bek was a great builder, being responsible for an even grander Great Hall on the west side of the Inner Bailey,

The Great Hall in the 1970s; although the Hall has been much altered, one of Bek's (shorter) windows survives in the south west corner.

over the Undercroft to the original Norman Hall. Even this did not satisfy Bishop Thomas Hatfield (1345–81), who enlarged the Hall by extending it southwards. He also made it much lighter (and less defensible) by inserting huge windows at both ends of the Hall and enlarging most of the remainder. This Hall became known as the Bishop's Hall (with le Puiset's range known thereafter as the Constable's Hall), and in it he is said to have had two thrones, emphasising his position as both spiritual and temporal ruler of the Palatinate.

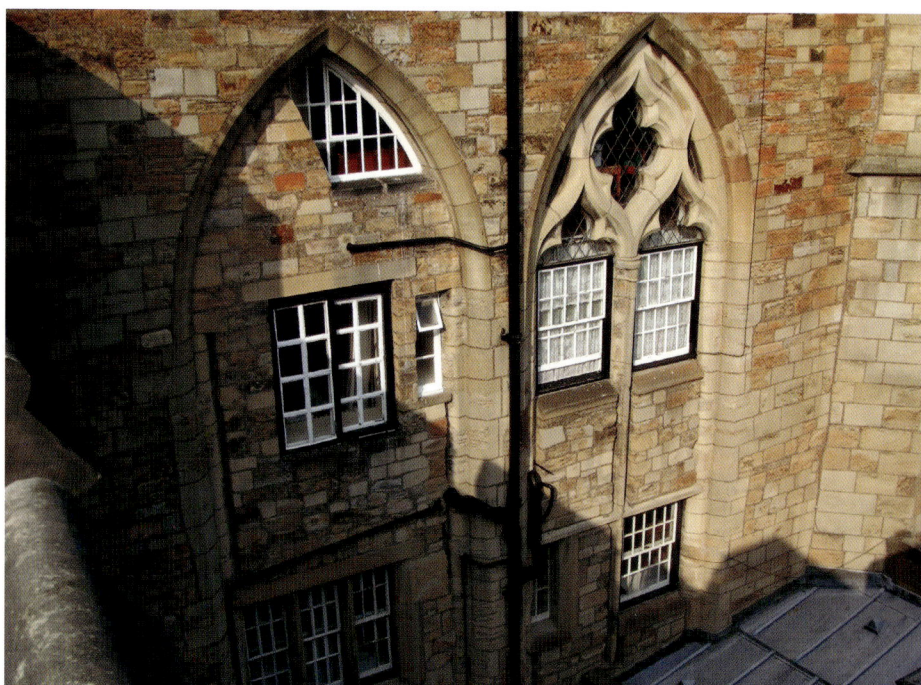

The south wall of Hall Stairs, showing the outline of the windows in Hatfield's enlarged Hall.

The remains of the Bastion tower of *c.*1300, photographed in the 1980s.

Bek may also have built the large bastion tower on the wall running north-east from the Keep to the North Gate. The upper parts of the Bastion collapsed in 1774, but enough remains for its general appearance to be conjectured.

Twice during the time of the following Bishop, Richard Kellaw (1311–16) the Scots raided Northumberland and reached the suburbs of Durham. In response to the incursions Edward II (1307–27) invaded Scotland in 1314, following his father's example, but was routed at Bannockburn – and in 1315 the Durham townsfolk, fearing further invasion, petitioned for, and received permission to 'levy murage', whereupon a defensive wall was rapidly constructed enclosing the Market Place to the north of the Castle.

Kellaw's successor, Bishop Lewis de Beaumont (1318–33), however, seems to have been less alarmed,

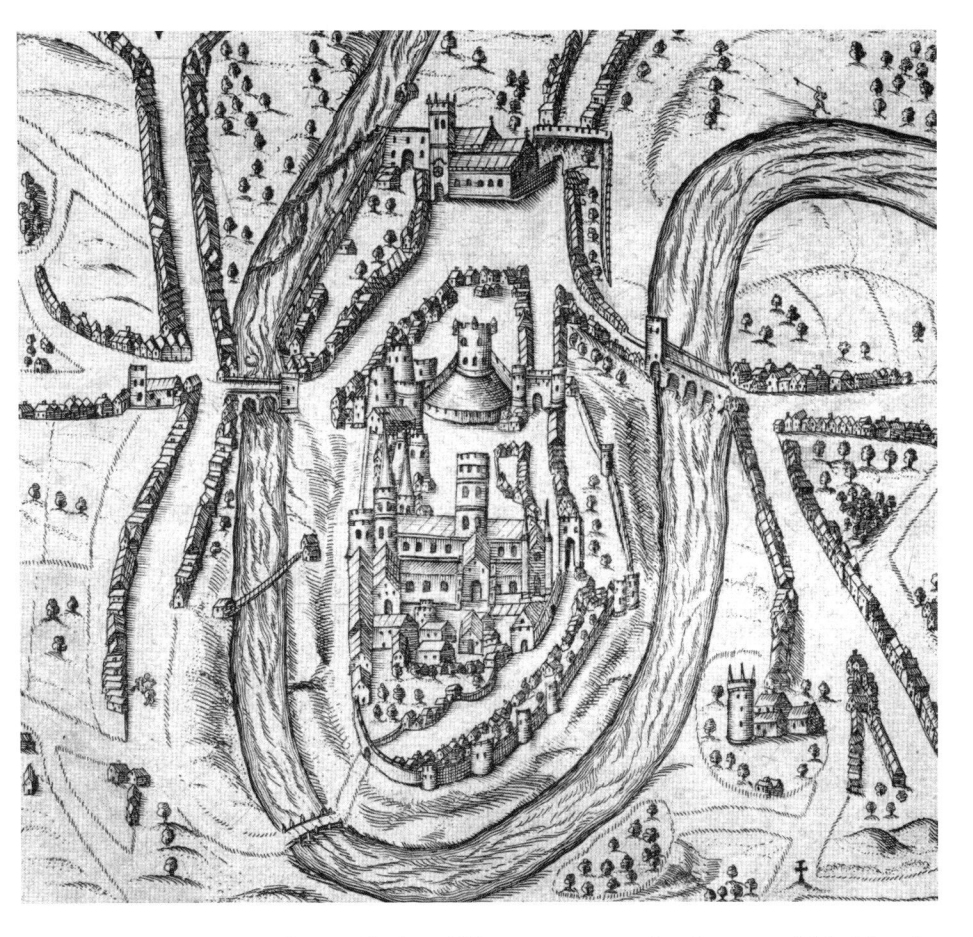

Speed's map of Durham, 1611, showing Hatfield's Keep and the city's defensive screen.

for he was chided by the King for neglecting the Castle's defences, after which he instituted a programme of repairs that included Flambard's wall running from the Castle to the Cathedral.

Less than a generation later, in October 1346, in the early years of the Hundred Years War between England and France and just one year into the episcopate of Hatfield, Durham was once more involved in the Scottish wars. With King Edward III (1327–77) otherwise occupied in France, David II of Scotland took the opportunity to invade northern England, but was brought to battle at Neville's Cross, a mile to the west of Durham. There Hatfield, another great warrior Bishop, played his part in the rout of David's army by the English barons.

Hatfield was also responsible for rebuilding the Keep in stone. The strengthening of the Castle's fortifications was probably seen as a necessary move, for David's invasion had made it clear that there was still the need for a defensive capability. Up to this time the Keep had been a fairly primitive wooden structure set within a stone curtain wall. It is not known what accommodation, if any, it contained, except that there was (in the mid-12th century at least) a dungeon beneath it.

The new building, roughly octagonal in shape, was a four-storey 'shell keep', meaning that rooms lined the inner side of the wall, leaving the centre open to the sky – and although the Keep was reconstructed in 1840 for the University it retains Hatfield's octagonal design and probably also a proportion of the original stone.

In order to enlarge the Keep it was, unfortunately, necessary to widen the mound, which now abutted directly against the east end of the Norman 'Chapel', thereby blocking the three east windows which were the building's principal source of light.

It was also Hatfield who replaced the roof of le Puiset's north range with a high-pitched open timber roof (the old, shallower, roofline is still visible) and added the large 14th-century window high up in the west wall of the range, above the Norman windows of the upper Hall. By implication, it may also have been he who first inserted a ceiling in the Upper Hall (the Norman Gallery), thus creating another gallery above it – for the window provides the only light in the otherwise-blind topmost gallery.

'The south view of Durham Castle, being the Bishop's palace', after S and N Buck, 1728. Note particularly Bishop Hatfield's 'Shell Keep' and the high-pitched roof on the North Range; also the Bastion tower (attributed to Bishop Bek) on the right below the Keep. A turret in the north west angle of the Courtyard (in the position now topped by the flag pole, but destroyed by 16th-century alterations) marked both the Norman and 14th-century entrances, accessible via a wooden stairway and a drawbridge.

'A north west view of the Castle from a field called the Hollow Croft above Framwelgate', issued with Forster and Mynde's Plan of Durham, 1754. The Keep, virtually windowless to the north, dominates the scene. Visible in the centre of the picture are Bishop Hatfield's window at the west end of the North Range and his north window in the Great Hall.

The south side of the North Gate *c.*1800 (from an unsigned oil painting in the Castle's collection). The North Gate, which also served as the county gaol, was demolished in 1820. Note the steep gradient of Saddler Street as it passed through the gateway.

Chapter Three
Durham Castle as a Palace

[1] The 15th Century

Early in the 15th century Bishop Thomas Langley (1406–37) made the last significant addition to the strength of the fortress, rebuilding the North Gate, the main entrance to the Outer Bailey of the Castle. This gate was massively defended:

'There was originally a main tower, and a barbican crossing the moat [which ran along the north side of the Castle], with its entrances defended by turrets. The gates were double, and there was a portcullis on the side facing the city, and probably one on the other side as well. On the north front were two large turrets, and on the south there was certainly one turret, and there were probably two. The passage between the gates was vaulted, there was a drawbridge within the barbican, and probably another outside.' (Whiting, 1933)

Both the Castle and the town were now better defended than they had ever been. Subsequent alterations to the Castle and the surrounding buildings were mostly made for different reasons, sometimes to make them more imposing but frequently also to increase the levels of comfort and convenience for both the Bishop and his guests. Over the centuries that followed, however, the Castle became more and more obviously a Palace, a residence befitting the status of the Prince Palatine, from which he could dominate the region and in which he could entertain on a lavish scale. The Castle's role as a fortress, however, diminished only gradually, so it was a while before the changes were allowed to compromise defensive capability.

The Castle's walls had not, of course, protected the area against the Black Death that hit Durham along with the rest of the country in 1349 and 1350, nor against subsequent outbreaks of plague early in the 15th century. The reduction in population as a result of these epidemics inevitably brought changes to the region. Landowners in particular had to make adjustments, since fewer people meant a reduction in rental income and, at the same time, rising costs – for labour was now in short supply, and the wages (and general well-being) of the 'lower orders' increased as a consequence. Life in the Castle, however, does not seem to have been greatly affected, perhaps because any shortfall in the Bishop's rent-roll was compensated for by his income from coal and other minerals.

It was probably Bishop Langley's successor, Robert Neville (1438–57), who built the Exchequer building, immediately outside the south-west corner of the Castle abutting the moat (the latter already rendered all but redundant by the strength of the outer defences). Although not therefore part of the

The Kitchen and Buttery in early 20th-century postcards. Note the ancient tables and the elaborate brick breastwork, the latter said to be the earliest use of brick in (Co.) Durham.

Detail of the wooden hatches in the Buttery with Fox's date, 1499, on the surround. The legend Est Deo Gratia (Thanks be to God) was perhaps intended to take the place of a spoken grace in Hall; the inscription is matched by similar work at Auckland Palace.

Durham Castle as a Palace

The Exchequer Building and the Castle entranceway. The arms are those of Bishop Neville (1438–57).

Castle itself, the building is worth mentioning, for it was one of considerable importance, containing not only the Bishop's Exchequer (the treasury and accounts department) but also the Chancery (the law court). The Bishop's mint, incidentally, had been established in 1135 by Bishop Geoffrey Rufus (1133–40) on a site on the north-east corner of Palace Green now occupied by student rooms and today known, appropriately enough, as Moneyers Garth.

Late in the 15th century Bishop Richard Fox (1494–1501) opted firmly for comfort, greatly reducing the length of the Great Hall in order to insert four floors of chambers at its south end beyond the Screens Passage (and thereby doing away with Hatfield's extension). The two Trumpeters' Pulpits (forerunners of the more extensive Minstrels' Gallery added by the University) at the south end of the reduced Hall were probably added at this time. Further rooms (now removed) at the north end of the Hall may also have been Fox's work, though these are normally ascribed to a much later Bishop, Richard Neile (1617–27).

Fox also remodelled the service buildings and servants' quarters to the south-west of the Great Hall, the most impressive work being in the Kitchen. The Castle's kitchens were probably always on the present site – the remains of ovens and a brew-house on the floor below the present Kitchen suggest as much – but Fox massively increased their capacity, for his Kitchen included three enormous stone fireplaces, one against the east wall and the other set two into the south wall of the Norman building. A large doorway and wooden hatches in the north wall gave easy access to the Buttery and thence to the Great Hall.

Fox's emblem in the Screens passage; a pelican piercing her breast to feed her young, a medieval symbol of the Eucharist.

Bishop Fox was very active both politically and militarily. Durham and the border still needed to be protected, most particularly in 1496, when James IV of Scotland invaded Northumberland in support of one of the pretenders to the throne of Henry VII (1485–1509), the first of England's Tudor dynasty. Once a truce had been signed between the two countries Fox also brokered the marriage alliance between James IV and Henry's daughter, Princess Margaret, and (as Bishop of Winchester) he entertained the Princess in Durham Castle while she was on her way north to her wedding in 1503.

[2] The 16th Century

Durham's peace was short-lived, for in 1513 Henry VIII (1509–47) invaded France and the Scots under James IV took the opportunity to invade northern England. The Bishop of Durham, Thomas Ruthall (1509–23), was with Henry when the Scots invaded his see, but he rushed back to Durham and his forces were prominent in the battle that followed. The Scottish army was routed at Flodden and James was killed, leaving as his successor his infant son James V. Although a disaster for the Scots, for Durham this appeared to signal peaceful times ahead, as the threat of invasion receded.

More turmoil was to follow, however, for the Reformation (the 16th-century movement that attempted to reform the Roman Catholic Church and led to the establishment of the various Protestant Churches) was a time of great religious and political upheaval for both the city and the nation as a whole. The 1530s in particular were to bring great changes to Durham.

Portrait of Bishop Fox (1494–1501).

Fox is said to have planned the conversion of Hatfield's Keep, to provide yet another hall, kitchen and other apartments, but his translation to Winchester in 1501 put paid to these ideas. He is also sometimes credited with sub-dividing the Lower Hall in le Puiset's range by inserting a floor across what is now the Senior Common Room at the level of the Senate Lobby and the Bishop's Suite – but there is little supporting evidence for this claim. He may well have remodelled the North Halls to some extent, however, for the both the (now-hidden) windows in the south wall of the Senior Common Room and its now Gothicised ceiling look 15th century in origin and could well be his.

Looking north east across the Courtyard to (from right to left) the Chapel, Bell-tower and Galleries built for Bishop Tunstal (1530–59).

Durham Castle as a Palace

On the national stage, Henry VIII obliged the clergy to recognise him as Supreme Head of the Church of England (confirmed by the Act of Supremacy of 1534) and he ordered the Dissolution of the Monasteries (1536–39). Durham's monastery surrendered to the Crown at the end of 1539 (and the Bishop may not have been wholly sad to see the back of the Prior, his rival within Durham City), but the revenues were restored to the church in May 1541 and the Cathedral entrusted to a Dean and Chapter (the last Prior and 12 former monks).

Meanwhile, the powers and privileges of the Bishop of Durham were being steadily eroded by the Crown, most obviously by the Jurisdiction of Liberties Act of 1536. This Act removed the Bishop's right to administer civil and criminal law; the power to appoint judges, coroners and sheriffs; and the privileges of collecting taxes and minting coins. The Bishop's courts continued to operate, but from that time onwards judges were appointed, and justice was administered, in the name of the King rather than of the Prince Bishop.

In the same year, 1536, many of the Palatinate's leading families joined in the northern English rebellion now known as the Pilgrimage of Grace. The main demand was for a reunion with the Church of Rome, but in Durham there was also a call for the restoration of the 'Liberties' of the Palatinate (presumably a reference to the Bishop's loss of judicial independence). Bishop Cuthbert Tunstal (or Tunstall, 1530–59), however, was not involved: he had (rather reluctantly) supported the Supremacy of the King, and fled to his Castle at Norham until the rebellion had been defeated.

The change in the Bishop's status was demonstrated for all to see at the trial of the rebels that followed:

Bishop Tunstal's Chapel.

a grand assize was held at Durham in March 1537, but it was presided over by the Duke of Norfolk as the King's representative, with Bishop Tunstal taking only a subordinate role. In the same year the Prince Bishop's powers were eroded still further, with the election of the Council of the North to govern the four northern counties of England in the King's name. The first president was, however, Bishop Tunstal, perhaps some compensation for the Bishop's loss of personal authority.

The years that followed saw see-sawing changes of religion under Henry VIII's children – Protestantism under Edward VI (1547–53); the return to Roman Catholicism under Mary (1553–58); and Protestantism once again under Elizabeth (1558–1603). Bishop Tunstal survived the reign of Edward, though he stood in the way of the ambitions of the Duke of Northumberland to rule the north and (perhaps because of this) was imprisoned in late 1551 and, ten months later, deprived of his see. Following the Duke's suggestions, an Act of Parliament of March 1553 abolished the Palatinate and claimed the revenues for the Crown: the intention was to replace the Prince Bishop with salaried Bishops of Durham and Newcastle (posts eventually created in 1836 and 1884, respectively).

Before the Act could be brought into effect Edward died and was replaced by his Catholic half-sister Mary, despite the Duke of Northumberland's efforts to install a Protestant Queen (his daughter-in-law, Lady Jane Grey). The Act abolishing the Palatinate was annulled in November 1553 and Tunstal was restored to his position.

During these years, so far as Durham Castle itself is concerned, Bishop Ruthall (1509–23) does not appear to have made any significant changes, and his successor, Thomas Wolsey (1523–29) never even visited the city, but under Tunstal in the 1530s and 40s the building underwent something of a transformation.

Portait of Cuthbert Tunstal, Bishop of Durham 1530-59.

His main additions are immediately apparent from the Gatehouse: he built a new Chapel in the north-east corner of the Courtyard; a new stairway, enclosed in a projecting bell-tower, giving access to the Chapel from the Courtyard; a two-storey Gallery, running along the length of the south wall of le Puiset's North Hall; and he altered the Gatehouse itself, widening the entrance, resetting its Norman archway and installing the massive iron-bound gates (and postern gate).

Bishop Tunstal's arms. His device of three combs on the right of the shield can be seen on the lower walls of the Bell-tower (see page 33 and above) and of the Gallery.

Tunstal's upper Gallery provided a grand passageway linking the Great Hall and the north range and the Chapel. Although essentially a lean-to against the earlier building, the Galleries added greatly to the comfort and convenience of the inhabitants and at the same time provided useful buttressing of le Puiset's building. The ornate entrance to le Puiset's lower Hall was now enclosed within Tunstal's upper Gallery, and the stairway approaching it had been removed. It had, in any case, presumably ceased to be the main entrance to the Castle with the construction of Bek's Great Hall some two centuries previously.

The Chapel was partly furnished with richly-carved woodwork brought by Tunstal in 1547 from the upper chapel at Auckland Palace. These furnishings included the seats at the west end of the Chapel as well as the pairs of stall-ends beneath the organ screen and below the altar. The stall-ends at least are early 16th century, since

Carved stall-ends in the Chapel; the one on the opposite page inadvertently reversed the design, since the cross and four lions of the bishopric should appear on the left and the arms of the individual Bishop on the right (as viewed).

they display the arms of Bishop Ruthall. The seats include misericords, or 'mercy seats': hinges allowed them to be folded back to the wall so that the congregation could stand, but a small projection on the underside of each seat allowed something a prop for those standing during an overlong service. This explains why many of the seats are intricately carved on their undersides (only).

Misericords in the Chapel. The whimsical carvings include a pig playing the Northumbrian pipes (an image repeated in a number of northern churches and said to be by the Ripon school of carvers); and a man wheeling his wife in a barrow.

THE SOUTH-EAST VIEW OF BISHOP-AUKLAND-PALACE, IN THE BISHOPRICK OF DURHAM.

To the Right Revd Father in God William Talbot Lord Bishop of Durham; Lord Lieut of this County; one of the Governours of the Charter House &c. The present Owner of this Palace; This Prospect is humbly Inscribed by Your Lordships most Obedt & Dutifull Servt S. & N. Buck.

Anthony Beck Bp. of Durham built a Palace here in K. Edwd. 1st Reign, who placed in it a Dean & Prebenderys, to whom he alow'd ye large Quaderangle for their Habitation. Walter Skirlaw, Lawrence Booth, & Thos. Ruthal succeeding Bps. made so considerable additions to it y'it became a most beautifull & Stately Building, which so much exasperated ye envious Rebels, that Sr Arthur Haslerig & his Men quite destroy'd it, Lying in its Ruins till Dr Jno. Cosins being made Bp. of Durham by K. C. 2. rebuilt, & magnificently adorn'd this decayed Palace, adding there to a Stately Chappel, A.D. 1667. in which he lies buried.

Saml & Nathl Buck delin et Sculpt 1728.

Auckland Palace in 1728, by S and N Buck.

Mention of Auckland Palace is a reminder that Durham Castle was merely the most politically-important residence of the Prince-Bishop. The Palatinate's holdings included properties as far north as Norham on the Tweed and as far south as Crayke, about 10 miles north of York. The Bishop's castle at Norham has already been mentioned; Stockton Castle was also his, as was Bishopton Castle, about 14 miles south of Durham. He also possessed a number of manor houses, including those at Darlington, Wolsingham (in Weardale) and Crayke; and there was even a Hunting Lodge, at Westgate in Upper Weardale. Auckland Palace, the bishop's country residence about 9 miles south-west of Durham, was begun in the 12th century and is even now the Bishop's Palace. Yet another residence, at Bishop Middleham, some eight miles south of Durham, appears to

THE SOUTH-EAST VIEW OF NORHAM CASTLE.

To William Orde Esq.r Owner of This Castle This Prospect is humbly Inscrib'd by His obliged humble Serv.ts S. & N. Buck.

THIS Castle was built by Ralph Bp. of Durham, on the top of a steep Rock moted round & fortefy'd with several strong Walls, for the better security of this part of his Diocess against the frequent incursions of the Scotch Moss=Troopers; it being on the Brink of the River Tweed Bordering Scotland, It hath often been of great service to England agst. the Scots, who were ever at War together, so that the English kept it very well fortefy'd; In the Reign of K.H.7. the K. of Scots besieg'd this Castle for many days, until he dispair'd of a Conquest, rais'd his Siege, & retreated: & in K.H.8. Reign James 5.th of Scotland attacked it with 10000 men, but the Governour wanting Amunition, after 6 Days brave resistance surrender'd it to the K. but was soon regain'd by the E. of Surry, who was afterwards created D. of Norfolk, & L.d Howard his son E. of Worcester. S. & N. Buck delin. et sculp.t 1728.

Norham Castle in 1728, also by S and N Buck.

have been the Bishops' preferred home until the 14th century, after which they transferred their affections to Auckland. By the time Tunstal's improvements were complete, Durham Castle was a vastly more convenient building for the Bishop and his retainers. Parts of it were, however, still somewhat primitive. Sanitation in Durham (as in every town) left a lot to be desired and in the Castle itself toilet facilities still consisted of *garderobes* set into the north and west walls from which the refuse went only as far as the ground below – another good reason for a Bishop with a sense of smell to prefer his country residence! Tunstal did, however, provide the Castle with additional fresh water, to supplement that provided by the well in the Courtyard, by tapping into the spring-fed supplies in the Cathedral close and running a lead pipe across the Green to the Castle.

The Keep, which was unimproved since Hatfield's time, was increasingly redundant and by now little-used: the strength of the outer fortifications meant that there was little need for a sizable military garrison to be maintained within the Castle, and any military presence could in any case be accommodated within the Constable's Hall. Similarly, since the construction of the North Gate, the dry moat on the south side of the Castle now performed little function other than as a convenient dump for refuse.

Few alterations were made to the Castle in the latter half of the 16th century, perhaps partly because they were deemed unnecessary but also because of the prevailing mood of the times: during the reign of Elizabeth church-folk, Tunstal's successors included, were rather more pre-occupied with stripping churches of unnecessary embellishments than with beautifying church property.

In addition, it was another period of general impoverishment in the region, partly a result of the failure of the Rising of the North in 1569, another attempt to restore the Catholic religion and to place on the throne a Catholic monarch, Mary, Queen of Scots (daughter of James V and granddaughter of Margaret Tudor) instead of her cousin, the Protestant Elizabeth. In the absence of Bishop Pilkington (1561–76), who fled to London, the Earls of Northumberland and Westmorland took over Durham, but their short-lived rebellion was suppressed in a matter of days and was followed by reprisals and the confiscation of the estates of many local landowners. In the past such estates (which included Westmorland's castles at Brancepeth and Raby) would have passed to the Bishop, but now they passed to the Crown by Act of Attainder, further hastening the decline in the Bishop's power.

[3] The 17th Century

In the 17th century the military function of Durham Castle all but vanished: although the formal Treaty of Union between England and Scotland would come only in 1707, Durham's most significant role, as a border fortress, was removed at a stroke in 1603 by the union of the English and Scottish crowns under James I and VI (son of Mary Queen of Scots and great grandson of Margaret Tudor), the first Stuart King of England. In addition, more modern methods of warfare, and in particular the development of more powerful cannons, were to render such fortresses increasingly obsolete. The Castle's role as a ceremonial palace continued, however, since the Bishop remained an important figure in the region despite the gradual erosion of his powers.

The elaborate overmantel in the Senate Suite; the arms of King James I (in the centre) are flanked by those of Bishop James.

The Castle had already received a number of royal visitors over the centuries (including King John in 1216; King Henry III in 1255; Alexander of Scotland in 1272; Edward III in 1334; and Princess Margaret in 1503) – but now the visits became more frequent. James I (1603–25) came to Durham both on his way to his English coronation in 1603 and again in 1617 – and in the Senate Suite there is now a fine fire surround, bearing the arms of both King James I and Bishop William James (1606–17), perhaps produced specifically for the royal visit in 1617 (though it was probably made for the old Exchequer building and installed in the Castle only in the 1850s).

By this stage, after more than half a century of relative neglect, the Castle seems to have been in need of some refurbishment: Bishop Neile (1617–27) is said to have found the buildings in great decay, and to have spent considerable sums on restoration work. If the space now occupied by the Senate Room had once been the Chapel, it had been redundant since the building of Tunstal's Chapel in the 1540s – and Bishop Neile is said to have re-modelled this part of the Castle (the east end of the north range) to create what is now known as the Senate Suite. In addition, he either built or remodelled the stack of rooms at the north end of the Great Hall, rooms which may have been accessed from a turret built by Tunstal (though, if so, all trace of the turret was removed when the Black Staircase was constructed in the 1660s).

Charles I (1625–49) was entertained in the Castle both on the way to his Scottish coronation in 1633 and again in 1639; he also passed through Durham in less happy circumstances as a prisoner of the Scots in 1647; and James II (1685–88) also visited.

The royal visit of 1639, during which Bishop Morton (1632–59) entertained the Monarch, was prompted by preparations for what are known as the Bishop's Wars (1639 and 1640): the Scottish Covenanters were threatening invasion and the Bishopric mustered men to attempt to repulse them. An agreement was patched up in 1639 and then broken by Charles, whereupon the Scots invaded and the English army fled. Morton also left Durham, never to return, and the Scottish general, Leslie, occupied the Castle until 1641.

Bishop Thomas Morton (1632–59).

During the Civil War between Crown and Parliament that began in 1642 and the Commonwealth period that followed, the Castle suffered badly, albeit from neglect rather than any military bombardment. After the Parliamentarian victory at Marston Moor in 1644, the Scots again occupied Durham, and stayed for three years.

Following the surrender of the King in 1646 the new order, led by Oliver Cromwell, immediately abolished the Bishopric and began to sell off church land. The Castle was bought by Thomas Andrews, Lord Mayor of London, in 1649, though he appears never to have visited and to have sold it on almost immediately to a Mistress Blakiston. In 1650, after the Battle of Dunbar, several thousand Scottish prisoners were held in the Cathedral, but many hundreds were dying from dysentery and the Castle was pressed into service as a make-shift hospital.

On the Restoration of the Monarchy in 1660 the Bishopric was also restored, but the new Bishop, John Cosin (1660–72) found the Castle and his other residences in a very sorry state. Durham Castle appears to have been uninhabitable, the Bishop commenting that it had been spoiled and ruined by the Scots with gunpowder. Cosin therefore devoted much of his time and the still-considerable revenues of the Palatinate to the restoration of his residences (as well as to the Cathedral and many other buildings within his diocese), and his successor, Nathaniel Lord Crewe (1674–1722) made further alterations during his long tenure of the see.

Most of the 17th-century work in and around the Castle accordingly belongs to the Restoration period under Cosin and to a lesser extent Crewe and (since the Castle also had to be largely re-furnished) virtually all of the surviving furniture, pictures and other adornments date to this time or later. Under Cosin the Castle required, and received, a huge amount of general repair work – but he also found the time and money to make what were be the last substantial additions to the fabric of the Castle. As a result, the buildings underwent another transformation, both inside and out.

The Black Stairs, built for Bishop Cosin in the 1660s, drawn in the later 19th century by JR Brown.

The view from Palace Green altered radically: Cosin demolished the Barbican and filled in the dry moat, since they were both by now redundant, replacing them with a wide driveway flanked by gardens (the present Fellows' and Master's Gardens). The Keep was also disused and obsolete, and its mound was landscaped to provide more gardens and three level terrace walks, the middle level leading around the mound onto the newly-created North Terrace, below which yet more garden ran down to the Castle's outer walls (above Moatside Lane).

Within the Courtyard, Cosin's hand is again immediately apparent. His most ambitious project was the imposing new stair-tower in the north-west corner of the Courtyard, containing within it the elaborately-carved staircase now known (from the colour of its woodwork) as the Black Stairs. Originally a cantilever, or 'flying' staircase, it appears to have settled quite rapidly and massive vertical oak columns were added to support it, perhaps within a decade of its construction.

The north west corner of the Courtyard, by RW Billings, c.1840. Cosin's Stair Tower is in the centre.

A later 17th-century oil painting of Constantinople (Istanbul), from the Castle Museum's collection, showing the possible source of inspiration for Cosin's additions to the Great Hall.

Tunstal's Chapel was refurbished (with the addition of new screens) and extended. The original position of the high altar is indicated by a piscina, an alcove for washing the communion vessels, that still exists behind the modern panelling – but at this period the east end was taken down and reconstructed one bay further to the east, retaining Tunstal's original east window. It was probably Cosin who started this work and his successor, Crewe, who completed it, since the coats of arms of both Bishops occur a number of times on the beams of the roof and elsewhere. The new work is much rougher than the old, almost certainly because it was intended that the stonework would be hidden beneath painted plaster.

Cosin also added a Porch in front of the original door of the Great Hall (though he retained Bek's entranceway within it); he refaced the building in the south-west corner of the Courtyard; and he strengthened both the buttresses along the Hall's east wall and the walls of the Keep mound. A lead-lined drinking-fountain mid-way along the eastern side of the Courtyard is also his; and during his time the well in the Courtyard (and Tunstal's additional pipe-fed supplies) became obsolete after he constructed a new conduit to carry water across the river from Elvet Moor to the Cathedral and Castle.

Inside the Castle, Cosin's Staircase made communication between the west and north ranges rather easier. He also lavished attention on the Great Hall, installing panelling throughout (since removed and replaced) as well as a screen at the south end and an audience chamber at the north end.

The Great Hall, facing South, c.1836. A rare image, attributed to Edmund Hastings (1781–1861), of the Great Hall before the removal of the 17th-century panelling.

Durham Castle as a Palace

The Bishop had also by now lost much of his remaining judicial power (his judicial independence having already been removed in 1536 and Durham having been fully integrated into the Northern Circuit since early in the 17th century). The Bishop entertained the Judges on their periodic visits to the County to sit at the Assize Courts, and he (and latterly the University, with a financial contribution from the County Council) provided Lodgings for the Judges in the Castle until as late as 1971. Indeed, much of the adaptation and refurbishment of the State Rooms referred to below may have been inspired by the obligation to provide suitable accommodation for the Judges.

The Judges' visit to Durham Castle, 1913.

Portraits of Bishops Nathaniel, Lord Crewe and John Cosin.

When the Bishopric was restored in 1660, Cosin regained most of the privileges and revenues enjoyed by his immediate predecessors, though some were retained by the Crown and the Prince Bishop's power and prestige were further reduced as a consequence. Cosin, however, successfully resisted the growing demand for wider Parliamentary representation, claiming that this would threaten his 'power and prerogative'. Parliament had, in fact, already passed a Bill in 1642 granting two representatives each to the City and County of Durham, but (except for a brief period from 1654 to 1656) this provision had yet to be enacted and the Palatinate lands had been represented by the Bishop alone. The City and County finally gained this privilege after the death of Cosin in 1672 and before the preferment of Crewe.

Durham Castle: Fortress, Palace, College

[4] The 18th and early-19th centuries

Durham Castle's role as the principal ceremonial palace of the Prince Bishops was to continue throughout the 1700s and into the early decades of the 19th century. Lord Crewe in particular seems to have revelled in the ceremonial aspect of his position, if surviving images are anything to go by: oil paintings of the time depict the Bishop's ornate barge below the Castle on the River Wear, and his ceremonial coach, led by six black horses, drawn up in the Courtyard.

The shape and character of the Castle's buildings were largely established, however, and no further major additions were thought necessary. Bishops from the time of Crewe onwards therefore largely confined their interventions to renovation of the Castle's external walls and the remodelling of parts of the interior, especially the north range. It was probably Crewe, for instance, who reduced the width of le Puiset's Upper Hall (the Norman Gallery) by inserted a series of rooms along its north side, rooms perhaps intended to house servants within easy reach of the grander apartments below.

The Keep, once the last line of defence, was by this stage ruinous: Crewe undertook some repair work in 1714, probably merely in order to make the building safe, and for the same reason Bishop Thomas Thurlow (1787–91) demolished the upper storeys in 1789.

The Castle and Cathedral in *c*.1700, with the Bishop's Barge on the River Wear.

The Courtyard and (partly demolished) Keep of Durham Castle, 1808 by John Buckler (1770–1851).

Durham Castle from the south west, by S Hooper, 1774.

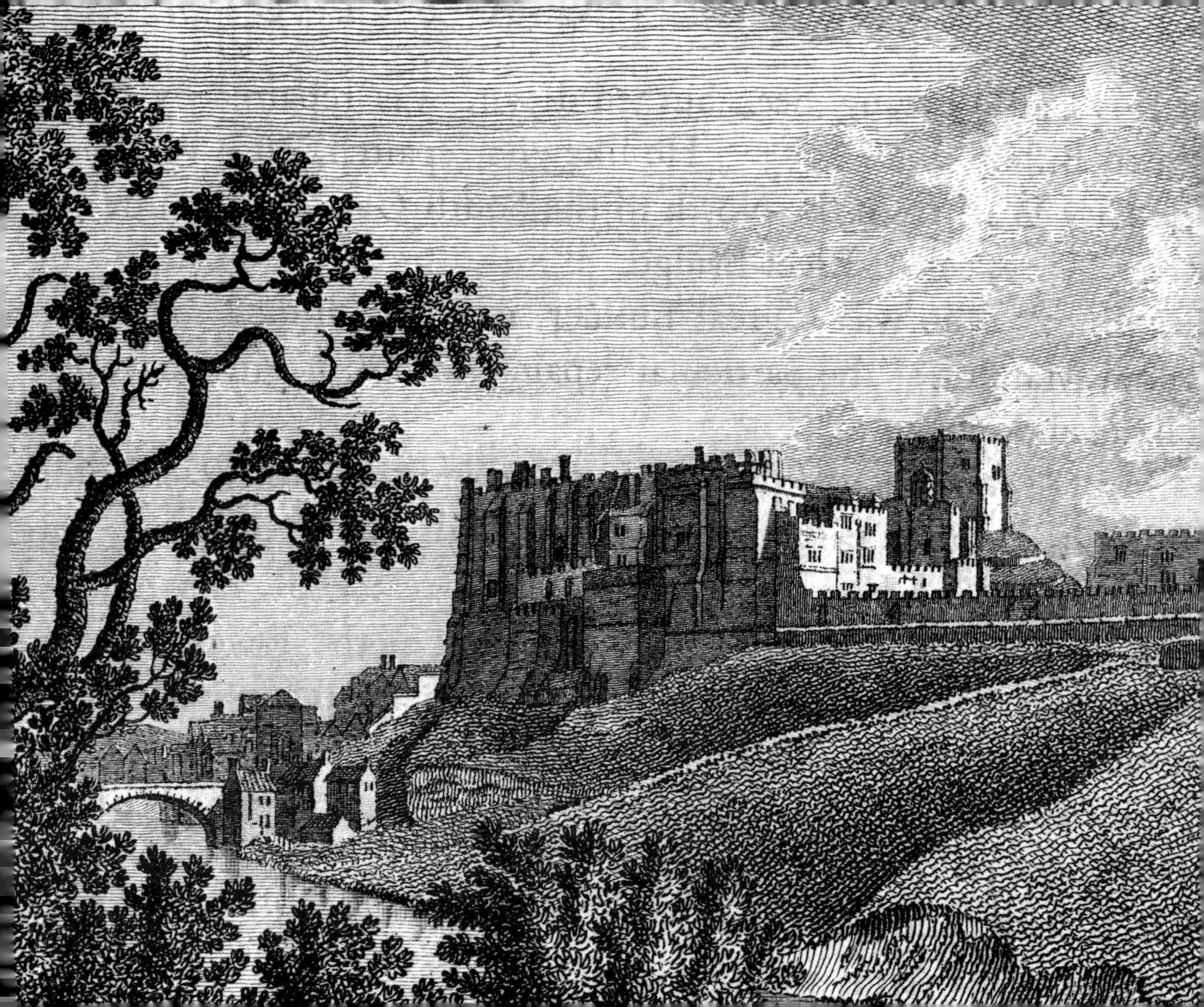

In the mid-18th century the exterior of le Puiset's Hall in the north range underwent substantial repairs and alterations, and its interior was re-modelled at the same time. This work was begun by Bishop Edward Chandler (1730–50) in the 1740s and continued by his successors Joseph Butler (1750–52), Richard Trevor (1752–71) and John Egerton (1771–87).

The north wall was partly rebuilt; the south wall, which was leaning outwards at an alarming angle, was cut back and refaced; and large beams both above the ceiling and beneath the floor of the Upper Hall tied the two walls together to arrest further movement. This work had the unfortunate effect of removing most of the Norman decoration on the outside of the windows on the Courtyard side of the Hall.

The arms of Bishop Butler (on the North Terrace).

The approach to the North Gate, by TM Richardson.

The North Gate, once the outermost defence, the main entrance to the Outer Bailey, was the last of the outer gates to survive. It was used as a prison until the early years of the 19th century (the deepest cells being well below street level), but was finally superseded by a new jail and demolished in 1820.

The arms of Bishop Trevor (on the south wall of the Norman Gallery). Gothic Revival 'ogee' arches (pointed arches with S-shaped curves to either side) similar to those in the SCR replaced the Norman decoration.

Inside the range, however, the Norman Gallery (all that remained of the Constable's Hall) was largely untouched and much of its decorative stonework survived. On the level below, the State Rooms took on their present form. The main room of le Puiset's lower Hall (now the Senior Common Room) was remodelled as an impressive Dining Room by the architect Sanderson Miller in the Gothic Revival style of which he was an early practitioner. The work was commissioned by Bishop Butler (after his only visit to Durham, in 1751) but cannot have been finished before his death in June 1752; and it was therefore completed under Bishop Trevor.

The Senior Common Room in the first half of the 20th century and in 2007. In the lower picture the funeral hatchment of Bishop Van Mildert (1826–36) is visible over the fireplace.

The sitting room of the Bishop's Suite.

The most important additions to the Dining Room were two enormous windows and a massive fireplace, all on the north side of the room. The room is still not well-lit, for its only daylight comes in through these two windows – but prior to this date the room must have very dark indeed: since the strength of the north wall had been an important element in the fortifications the main windows had faced south, but those windows had been blocked by the addition of Tunstal's Gallery some two hundred years previously.

The ceiling of the room must be considerably earlier (an addition, made in the 15th century or thereabouts, about a foot below the floor of the Norman Gallery) – but the 'Strawberry Hill Gothic' decoration was added at this the time – both the gilding around the edges and also the central ornaments (probably water lilies, but often described by members of the Senior Common Room as 'jam tarts').

At the west end of le Puiset's range, on a higher level, the suite of rooms now known as the Bishop's Suite also took on its current form: it too was remodelled for Bishop Trevor, whose arms appear over the rococo fireplace in the sitting room.

At the other end of the range, the Octagon Room was formed by Bishop Egerton. This was, and is, accessed from the anteroom to what we now call the Senate Suite. The latter was then a grand Withdrawing Room, with a bedroom beyond. The Senate Room already existed, but it took on its present look at this time with the addition (perhaps by Egerton) of a set of 17th-century Flemish tapestries illustrating scenes from the life of Moses.

The Anteroom to the Senate Suite.

The Octagon Room.

The refurbished State Rooms in the north range were undoubtedly impressive, but the furniture within them, it seems, was not: John Wesley, visiting in 1780, commented that *'many of the apartments are large and stately, but the furniture is mean beyond imagination'*. Despite the names attached to them, the Bishop probably made little use of these rooms, preferring when in residence the set inserted in the north end of the Great Hall by Fox or Neile. This explains the improvements made in the lower of these rooms, a dining room, by Bishop Egerton – and Henry Gee (Master, 1902–18) was probably correct in suggesting that, when the Assizes were held, suitable furniture was brought over from Auckland for the use of the judges.

The penultimate Prince Bishop, the Hon. Shute Barrington (1791–1826), was the last to turn his hand to alterations of the Castle. The Dean and Chapter commissioned the architect James Wyatt to pull down the Norman Chapter House of the Cathedral – but Barrington and Wyatt were kinder to the Castle, merely remodelling and partly reconstructing the Gatehouse and adjacent parts of the curtain wall in Gothic style.

The last Prince Bishops, the Hon. Shute Barrington (1791–1826) and William van Mildert (1826–36).

When Barrington died in 1826 at the age of 92, he was succeeded by Bishop William Van Mildert (1826–36). Up to this time Durham Castle remained the ceremonial centre of the Bishops' power, even though successive Bishops had mostly preferred Auckland Palace as a residence. Occasional grand events were still held in the Castle, one of the last and most memorable being a dinner hosted by Bishop Van Mildert on 3rd October 1827 for the Duke of Wellington, hero of Waterloo, and more than a hundred other distinguished guests. The *Durham Advertiser* reported that *'in the memory of no one present had so splendid an entertainment been seen in the Castle of Durham.'*

The Gatehouse by Joseph Bouet, 1828.

The Courtyard by J Deason, 1838 (prior to the reconstruction of the Keep).

Among the guests was Sir Walter Scott, who commented that *'The old Prelate contrived to sustain admirably the character of a Count Palatine with that of a Bishop'*. During the time of Van Mildert, however, there was increasing national agitation for the abolition of the remaining temporal powers of the church and for the redistribution of its excess income – and after Van Mildert's death in 1836 the remaining palatinate powers of the bishopric passed to the Crown.

Van Mildert was therefore the last Count Palatine, the last Bishop who could be styled 'Prince Bishop'. Future Bishops were appointed on a fixed income, and Auckland Palace became, and remains, both the Bishop's official residence and the administrative centre of the Durham diocese. Eighteen months after Van Mildert's passing, Durham Castle was handed over to the newly-established University of Durham, the subject of the next chapter.

The Courtyard and (newly rebuilt) Keep in the early 1840s, by RW Billings.

Chapter Four

University College and the University of Durham

[1] Establishing a University

The history of University College begins in the 1830s with the foundation of the University. However, nearly half a millennium before that, certainly from 1278 onwards, the Benedictine Abbey at Durham maintained a Durham Hall, or College, at Oxford, specifically designed as a training cell and intended to return learned monks to the mother house in the north. This arrangement, nurtured and funded by Durham for over 260 years, came to an abrupt end in 1544 following the surrender of monastic lands to the crown after Henry VIII's dissolution of the monasteries.

There were, however, plans to establish a College in Durham itself, connected to the Cathedral and funded out of the revenues of the dissolved monastery – but unfortunately the scheme was not carried through.

More than a century passed, to the 1650s and the Commonwealth era that followed the English Civil Wars and the execution of King Charles I. The Cathedral, Castle and College (as Durham's Cathedral Close is, rather confusingly, known) stood empty, since the Cathedral Chapter had been dissolved by Act of Parliament in April 1649 and the Puritan church then in the ascendant had no use for such elaborate buildings – and the site was handed over to a new Durham College. The intention was again admirable: this time to educate northerners in the north (rather than sending them south, perhaps never to return), so that they would be more likely to remain in the region and thus raise the general standard of education.

The Lord Protector, Oliver Cromwell, signed letters patent in May 1657, outlining the endowment, organisation, annual fees, and even naming members of staff of the new institution – but the project had not really got off the ground when the Restoration of 1660 restored not only the monarchy but also the whole hierarchy of the Church of England of which the monarch, Charles II, was the head. Thus the new Provost and Fellows (who had already taken possession of their houses) had to make way for the Bishop, Dean and Chapter – and another Durham College came to a premature end.

Another 170 years were to pass before the changing political climate finally brought the University of Durham into being, at the instigation of the Bishop, Dean and Chapter of Durham Cathedral. Their motives were perhaps less than pure, but the results were both admirable and enduring. As J.T. Fowler commented, a century ago:

'*They were fully alive to the need for such an institution in the North of England*' but '*there are signs also that the ecclesiastical body was influenced by a sort of panic at a time when all church property was in danger*'. [*Durham University, Earlier Foundations and Present Colleges*, 1904, 22–3].

This was a reference to the anti-clerical agitation that surrounded the discussions leading up to the 1st Reform Act, finally passed in 1832: church incomes were perceived to be excessive or at least ill-distributed, and the church authorities in Durham, certainly enjoying a very generous income, appear to have acted to make good use of some of the surplus before it was taken from them.

Nonetheless, the idea '*was in exact conformity with the principles on which they were themselves incorporated, the education of youth being enumerated among the objects of the Cathedral foundation, as set forth both in its charter and in its statutes.*' [ibid.]

In Durham we tend to date our foundation from 1832, but there are various significant dates, any one of which might be regarded as signalling the beginning of the University and that of University College, its foundation college.

The first, and arguably most significant steps, came in late September 1831: on 21st the Cathedral Chapter, at the instigation of the Dean (Dr. John Banks Jenkinson), proposed the setting up of an 'Academical Institution or College or University' at Durham; and a week later, on the 28th, the Chapter also accepted, with slight amendments, the Dean's initial plans for that institution, which laid out what subjects were to be taught; which staff were required; how many students there were to be; how it was all to be funded; and much more. Having established the basics, much of the detail was then worked out over a remarkably short period of time (at least it seems remarkable to those of us accustomed to modern university bureaucracy!), and they had even, by early December, provisionally appointed the first Warden (Principal), Archdeacon Charles Thorp.

Archdeacon Charles Thorp, 1st Warden of the University and Master of University College (c.1839–1862).

The next step was to gain the consent of Parliament. This was achieved in the following year, William IV granting the royal assent to the necessary Acts on July 4th, 1832. At that stage the University of Durham formally came into being – and accordingly we now take this to be our foundation date, even though the first University Calendar, published in the Autumn of 1833, makes rather more of the foregoing Act of Chapter than of the subsequent Acts of Parliament.

Archdeacon Thorp's original scheme for the new University (dated 9th December, 1831) stated that *'it is intended that the College, or University, be opened in October, 1832'*. However, it took a while to gets things moving, and it was only on July 20th, 1833 that Thorp was able to publish his *'Preliminary Arrangements'*, indicating that the first students would be admitted in the Michaelmas (Autumn) Term of 1833.

The first term actually began on 28th October, 1833 and ended on 18th December. Entrance examinations took place on the first day, with 19 foundation students (scholars) and 18 ordinary students being admitted. Many of the staff had already been appointed in time to be listed in the *'Preliminary Arrangements'*, and a full list of both staff and students was included in the first Calendar.

In the course of 1834 and 1835 the University's statutes were drawn up and agreed. The new institution was to be governed by the Dean and Chapter, with the Bishop acting as Visitor, while the affairs of the University were to be managed by the Warden, a Senate and a Convocation. The Senate was made up of a select few University academics, and the Convocation initially consisted of members of the University who held higher degrees (i.e. a Doctorate or Masters degree) from Oxford, Cambridge or Dublin. The Convocation was to be augmented by holders of Durham higher degrees, just as soon as some had been awarded.

The University was granted a royal charter by William IV on 1st June, 1837, and Durham's first degrees were conferred a week later, on 8th June: Thorp's original prospectus had announced that the period of education at Durham was to be four years and, although this was later to change, so it was that the initial intake of students in 1833 was graduating in 1837, at the end of their fourth year of study.

But what of the Hall of Residence for the students of this new University? There seems, at the outset, to have been no intention to hand over the Castle to the University – it was, after all, one of the Bishop's principal residences. Instead, there were plans for a range of university buildings (hall, common rooms, etc.) on the west side of the Palace Green – though it was only in June 1834 that the architect Anthony Salvin was instructed to draw up plans for this scheme.

In the meantime, also on 20th July, 1833, the Chapter had ordered that the foundation students (who were to be accommodated free of charge) were be housed in the Archdeacon's Inn, under the Bursar. This is the building on east side the Palace Green subsequently known as University House but now known as Cosin's Hall (the latter reviving the name given to it when it was briefly used as a separate Hall of Residence between 1851 and 1864). In August 1834 instructions were given for the enlargement of the 'University Hall' (probably the ground floor of the Inn) by the taking in of the Bursar's room, the rest of the building presumably being given over to individual student's sets.

This therefore appears to have been the University's first student accommodation block, housing the scholars, while it is not entirely clear whether the University provided rooms for the ordinary students in houses elsewhere or whether they had to find their own digs in the city. Lectures took place in various buildings around the Green, and, for morning

Students arriving for worship in the Chapel of the Nine Altars at the east end of the Cathedral.

prayers, the University had the use of either the Chapel of the Nine Altars (at the extreme eastern end of the Cathedral) or the Galilee Chapel (at the west end).

The standard of this accommodation can only be guessed at: rooms may, or may not, have been newly refurbished for the students, but by the late 1840s they seem to have left a lot to be desired: the cartoons of the Revd. Edward Bradley (see page 60 and 68), who graduated in 1848 ('Cuthbert Bede', of whom more below), make that quite plain. By that stage, however, alternative accommodation was available. The projected buildings on the west side of the Green never made it off the drawing board, but that was because all such plans had become superfluous when the University acquired the use of Durham Castle.

Bishop Van Mildert, who had presided over the beginnings of the University as Visitor, died in February 1836 and was replaced by Bishop Edward Maltby (1836–56). From Summer 1836 onwards, with the new Bishop's permission, the University began using parts of the Castle, principally the Great Hall and Tunstal's Chapel – and on 8th August, 1837, the whole building was formally handed over to the University. Initially the Castle was held in trust by the Bishop for the benefit of the University (ownership eventually being transferred by Act of Parliament to the Council of the Durham Colleges in 1908).

The Castle was immediately adapted to provide accommodation for students and staff. In particular, Bishop Hatfield's Keep, by then almost entirely ruinous, was rebuilt by Salvin in 1840 to provide student rooms – and those rooms are still in use today.

Bishop William van Mildert (1826–36).

Bishop Edward Maltby (1836–56).

The first of two sheets of cartoons of college life in the 1840s by Cuthbert Bede; showing a freshman's arrival at the old Gilesgate railway station (now defunct); staying overnight at the Waterloo Inn (next to Elvet Bridge); meeting with the Warden and Master, Charles Thorp; and looking for accommodation in University House (Cosin's Hall) before rejecting it in favour of the newly-rebuilt Castle Keep. (See page 68 for sheet 2.)

To start with, however, the label 'The University College' applied to all University accommodation, not just the Castle – and this situation continued until 1846 when a separate Hall was opened: a distinction could then be made between 'University College' (without the article) and 'Bishop Hatfield's Hall'. In addition, there was to start with no

The College Arms as they appear on the 1913 Grant of Arms.

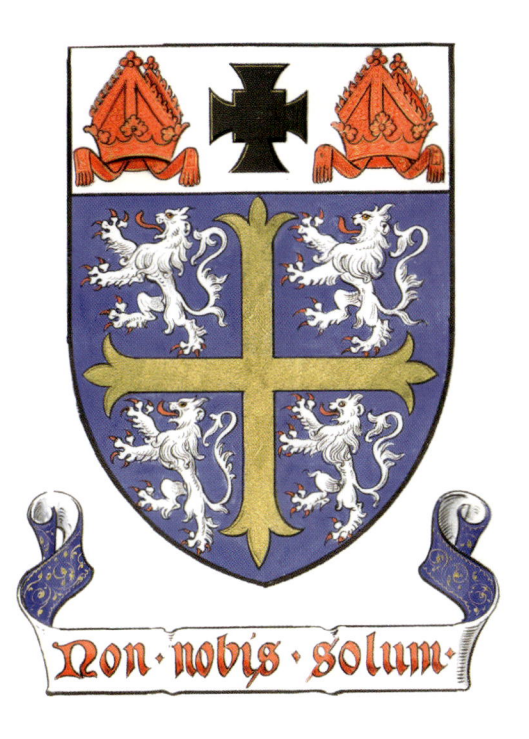

separate Master of University College: the Warden presided, as Warden, for the first couple of years, and was thereafter, until his death in 1862, styled Master as well as Warden (although a separate Vice-Master lived in the Castle).

There was thus no separate college foundation – and it was not until 1913 that University College obtained a separate Grant of Arms (something obtained by the University itself in 1843). This, incidentally, explains the slight variations in the arms used by the College at various times, there being for a long time no definitive design to follow. Despite these quibbles, however, the history of 'Castle' as part of the University can be said to have begun with its transfer on 8th August, 1837, and thus the latest stage of the Castle's story was underway.

The first two accommodation blocks: University House, or the Archdeacon's Inn (Cosin's Hall, now the Institute of Advanced Study); and, in the foreground, the Castle's Keep.

61

[2] The first 50 years (1830s–1880s)

Various details of the early Castlemen can be gleaned from the documents of the time: the Calendar names them (one John Cundill having the distinction of being listed as the first student to be enrolled); and it names the various Professors and Fellows, thereby also telling us which subjects could be studied – Divinity, Classics, Maths, Law, Medicine, History and Moral and Natural Philosophy. Charles Thorp's 1831 prospectus also itemizes the various categories of student:

Foundation students, having lodgings and a Table provided for them, free of expense;
Ordinary students, maintained at their own cost, but subject in all respects to the College Rules of Discipline, and to have every Academical Privilege in common with the other students;
Occasional students;
Divinity students.

According to Edward Pace, who contributed a short article on *University College and Hatfield College* to Whiting's *Durham University Centenary* volume (published in 1937), the constitution of the new university and its first college was probably modelled upon that of Christ Church, Oxford, of which Dr. Samuel Smith (a member of the Cathedral Chapter at the time of the University's foundation) had been the Dean. Despite being an Anglican foundation, however, Durham (unlike Oxford) never attempted to impose religious 'tests' on its students (though there was opposition in Chapter to allowing church endowments to benefit Dissenters).

Van Mildert, Thorp and the Dean and Chapter would all have had a clear sense of what a College for undergraduates should be like – and the essentially medieval buildings of Durham Castle were seen to be extremely appropriate for conversion into a traditional college on the 'Oxbridge' model. They could readily provide a large communal dining hall with supporting kitchen, public rooms suitable for a library and common rooms and commodious 'sets' for resident (male) students and (bachelor) dons.

The Revd John Cundill, first student of the University. This portrait, by Clement Burlison, dated 1889, hangs in the Great Hall.

BISHOP COSIN'S HALL—STUDENTS COMING FROM LECTURE

Students leaving lectures in Cosin's Hall in the early years of the University.

Lecture rooms were not required within the College, for the founders would not have expected the College to do much 'academic' teaching: that was the function of the professors appointed by the University. Lectures took place in various buildings elsewhere in the University and from the start were open to all students, not just the members of University College.

The founders would have expected the College to enforce a strict 'moral' policy of student manners and conduct: indeed, the 1837 University Calendar stated that *'The University College was formed for the purpose of uniting a system of domestic discipline and superintendence with academical instruction'*.

The original regulations of the University (reproduced in J.T. Fowler's *Durham University*, 1904) were quite strict and restricting. Attendance at lectures was compulsory, and so also was presence at breakfast and dinner in Hall, as well as at Chapel prayers or Cathedral service at the times appointed and at evening prayers in College. All students were expected to be in College before the gates were closed at night, and all visitors ('Strangers') had to leave before evening prayers. Finally, lights (oil, at this stage) were to be out by midnight, and the college servants, sometimes accompanied by the Censor, were to do the rounds to check that all were extinguished.

Academic dress had to be worn in public except 'in going to a gentleman's house more than two miles from Durham' or on the river. For rowing (a popular activity from the outset of the University), full academic dress was to be worn as far as the boathouse, and in the boat either an academical or boating cap (but *not* a hat).

Dice, cards, betting and gambling were all outlawed, and students were also forbidden to hire any room or house in the city, to frequent inns, public houses, or cooks' or confectioners' shops.

The Censor, the College Officer responsible for discipline, would note any absences with a cross in the Butler's book (the Butler being an influential figure both above and below stairs), and the student concerned was deemed to have 'lost' a day's residence. Ten such crosses meant the loss of a full term.

However, the reality of Durham life seems to have been somewhat less strict, for within a very few years, at least one rule had lapsed or was being regularly ignored, since many students took breakfast in their own rooms without suffering any official sanction. Other rules were also frequently flouted, the chief offences appearing to be the smuggling in of additional provisions; coming in after hours; the running up of excessive credit in local shops (especially for tobacco); and 'ragging' and generally rowdy behaviour.

Examination of the students of the University of Durham, October 1842, by RW Buss.

The original intention of the founding fathers of the University had been to provide a relatively inexpensive education for northern men at an all-inclusive charge, but it seems that the idea was rapidly subverted by the entry of the sons of a number of wealthy northern families, young men who could afford to live more luxuriously than their neighbours. This was somewhat unfortunate for the new University, for poorer families could not match the conspicuous expenditure of these students and many were thus deterred from sending their sons to Durham. Some went instead to Oxford or Cambridge, which, with the advent of the railways and the foundation of various scholarships, were becoming more accessible to northerners; others simply stayed at home – and student numbers at Durham thus remained very low.

The University reacted pragmatically: it made no attempt to dissuade the wealthy from attending Durham, but instead in 1846 founded a second Hall of Residence in North Bailey, Bishop Hatfield's Hall, for men of limited means. In the new Hall all meals were taken in common and all rooms were let furnished – while, across the way in the Castle, a slightly grander mode of life was allowed to continue. The new Hall successfully attracted students, but a further Hall, Cosin's Hall, utilising the University's original accommodation block in the Archdeacon's Inn, lasted only thirteen years (1851–64) because of lack of demand. Fowler's comment was that *'the money spent on it would perhaps have been better employed in enlarging Bishop Hatfield's Hall'*. [1904, 47]

Low student numbers continued to be a cause for concern, so much so that there was for a while in the late 1850s and 1860s a very real possibility that the University would close altogether. An Act of Parliament of 1861 set up a Royal Commission '*to enquire into the condition and prospects of the University and to make provision for an improved state of affairs*' – and on the 30th June 1862 the Commission issued a set of Ordinances for the reform of the University (one of them requiring the retirement of the elderly Thorp, by then nearly eighty). A further Act of Parliament (*The Durham University Act,* July 1864) authorized the Cathedral Chapter to submit plans to the Commissioners for the abolition of various fellowships, the moneys thus saved to be spent on the schools of Theology and Arts.

In addition, the Commissioners announced that the charges at Durham were excessive, and an Act of Chapter in 1865 therefore instructed the University Senate to find ways of reducing expenses. The Chapter also decreed (again in 1865) that the degree of B.A. could be taken after only two years instead of the previous three, thereby reducing students' costs.

Numbers coming to the University as a whole gradually began to pick up, but, even so, the number of students resident in author who contributed to various periodicals (including *Punch* and the *Illustrated London News*), producing a considerable body of work under the pseudonym 'Cuthbert Bede'. He was not, it must be admitted, a particularly distinguished churchman, but his writing and, especially, his drawings and cartoons, present a series of vivid and entertaining snapshots of student life in Durham in the 1840s.

His output included a number of images of life in and around Durham, not the least interesting being a little sketch, dated 1846, of the Castle complete with its newly-rebuilt Keep, viewed from the Cathedral bell tower.

The Revd Edward Bradley (1827–1889), alias Cuthbert Bede.

University College in the early 1870s was still only in the 20s (and as low as 22 in 1873).

Documents such as Thorp's prospectus, the University regulations and Acts of Parliament, however, give us only the dry bones of Castle life – and it is thus very fortunate that we have one or two less formal records of the formative years of the University with which to flesh out our picture.

One of the earliest students was one Edward Bradley, later the Revd. Edward Bradley. He (1827–1889) studied for his B.A. at University College, between 1845 and 1848 before going on to ordination and a career in the Church of England – but he was also a talented artist and

The Castle, Durham, sketched from the summit of the Bell Tower of the Cathedral January 1846, by Cuthbert Bede.

Staircase in the Castle of Durham (The Black Stairs)', by Cuthbert Bede.

Perhaps of even more interest, to Castlemen in particular, is Bradley's record of parts of the interior of the Castle: the Tunstal Gallery, looking essentially as it does today (though the tapestries shown on the north wall have now been removed to protect them from sunlight); and Bishop Cosin's staircase. The 'Black Stairs' appear brown: this could be artistic licence; but it may be that the watercolour has faded catastrophically; or, perhaps more likely, the stairs had yet to be stained black.

Yet more intriguing for Castlemen (and Norman Gallery residents in particular) are his images of a pair of rooms on that Gallery: a bed-sitting room and a dining room, both occupied in Bradley's final year by Frederick John Richards. These rooms were remodelled during the mid-1970s but are still occupied by undergraduates in term-time.

Several other images of Castle also exist, including 'Knocking In' at the Gatehouse. At that date the gates were locked at 10 pm, and latecomers either had to haul on the bell-rope and be prepared to explain themselves to the Warden the following morning, or they could try to climb in over the walls. Now that residents have their own keys the latter sport has long ceased, and even the bell-pull has disappeared in recent years.

Neither academic work nor sporting life escaped Bradley's attention: his series of etchings of College Life include 'revision' 1840s-style (probably in the Fellows' Garden, or perhaps in what is now the Master's Garden); and the Boat Club in 'training' by the fireplace in the Great Hall.

Best of all, however, are two sheets of cartoons, entitled *'Ye Fresshemonne His Adventures at University College, Durham'* (see pages 60 and 68). Bradley's most famous publication was an illustrated comic novel of university life,

An undergraduate Dining Room (off the Norman Gallery), by Cuthert Bede.

The Castle and Palace Green in the 1860s (from the *Illustrated London News*).

'The Cricket Match', drawn by Cuthbert Bede for the *Illustrated London News*, 1848.

'Knocking In' by Cuthbert Bede. This image was re-used in 'Verdant Green' as the gate of his imaginary 'Brazenface' College, Oxford.

'Reading for the June Examinations'.

The Boat club in 'training'. The University Crew after 11 months severe training.

The second sheet of Cuthbert Bede's Durham cartoons, charting the Freshman's revels after matriculation (acceptance into the University).

'*The Adventures of Mr. Verdant Green*'. The original cartoons for the latter were based upon life in Durham, but the publisher thought a book based on Durham would attract little interest, so the venue was switched to Oxford. Luckily, however, we still have the Durham cartoons, Bradley's comic record of life in College in the 1840s.

Other interesting insights into Castle life in the early years come from another Durham graduate, Charles Grey Grey, who entered the University in October 1842. He later wrote down and had privately published some reminiscences of Durham life (delightfully entitled *The Story of his Official Life*).

From him, for instance, comes confirmation that the rules on residence were not as strict as they at first appeared. Although at that early stage no student was allowed to take a degree until twelve terms (the equivalent of four years) had passed, he was, in fact, only required to keep nine. Grey Grey actually kept eleven, missing the Epiphany Term of 1845 altogether:

'I did not go up, professing to read at home, as I was changing from Engineering to Classics, though I spent much time hunting and otherwise amusing myself.'

He also confesses that life in the new Keep could be quite noisy:

'I fear he and I [his friend the Hon. Henry Douglas], who were chums in the keep, were sometimes rather noisy. The Reverend David Melville, a tutor, also lived near us, and was subject to fits of tertian ague. On one occasion he, knowing our habits, kindly sent for us and told us how he was suffering, and knowing we were the steadiest men in the keep, asked us to influence the rowdy men to keep

The Great Hall, looking south, by J Brown, as it appeared between the 1840s and the 1880s (i.e. without panelling).

quiet till he was well. We thought it a most kindly way of reproving us.'

More details come from the 1860s, in particular from a student signing himself 'P', who contributed his reminiscences (perhaps rendered slightly hazy by the passage of time) to the *Durham University Journal* in 1914.

From 'P' we gain anecdotes about various topics, including students and staff; the hazards of untended candles in student rooms (there is now a ban on candles but they were obviously essential then); and a College Choral Society, already going strong in the 1860s, though its Saturday evening concerts were relegated to 'the shades' (a gloomy room, presumably part of the Undercroft, under the dais at the north end of the Great Hall).

He, like all residents before and since, commented on the food, and, like all undergraduates before and since, was convinced (perhaps at this time with good reason) that the dons received special treatment:

'Plum pudding was a staple dish at the Castle dinner. What we did not eat used to be served up to us next day in slices fried and bore the name of 'Resurrection'. A student, on payment of threepence, was permitted to have sweets from the High Table, which were of superior class to those we got. It was not, however, considered good form to flaunt his wealth too often.'

Another subject that strikes a modern chord is that of students on the roofs. College Officers have always tried to dissuade students from mountaineering exploits, for fear of accidents, but students have seemingly always enjoyed the past-time:

'The more dangerous the roof, the more popular it was. Happily no one ever came to grief…'

Yet another subject for comment was the rivalry between Castlemen and the students of Hatfield Hall, a matter which has always perturbed the College authorities but has rarely given rise to serious problems:

'There was little acquaintanceship between the students, and I can remember one Castle man saying that he did not even know where Hatfield was until many years after he left Durham.'

The latter, however, was put into context by another correspondent who wrote in to say that this *'superior tone was merely a pose adopted by Castle men'* ('Sanex', *DUJ* 1915). Likewise, Whiting (1932) quoted Dr. Fowler as saying:

'I was at Hatfield from 1858 to 1861, and four of my best friends were Castlemen.'

It seems that life for many, if not most, Castlemen in the early years of the University, may have been a rather pleasant and comfortable experience – but that is not to say that life was entirely without problems, at least for the staff.

Most of the new University's staff were graduates of the Universities of Oxford or Cambridge, and many of Durham's ideas and practices were therefore based quite closely on those of the older institutions. However, the fledgling University did not have the sort of income which would allow its members to match the lifestyle enjoyed by Oxbridge dons, not least because the Church was still the major landowner in the Durham area, enjoying the sorts of rents and privileges that in Oxford and Cambridge accrued to the Colleges. The Castle, in particular, had been handed over to the University without an endowment for its up-keep (without which financial security the National Trust, for instance, would no doubt these days refuse to accept a similar property), and it was reliant upon further grants from the Cathedral authorities for any major items of expenditure.

It is to be supposed, therefore, that the University was often rather strapped for cash, as the following letter from Bishop Edward Maltby to Archdeacon Thorp seems to imply:

'I happened to dine with Mr. Justice Patterson yesterday at Archdeacon Watson's, for whom I preached a Charity Sermon and he was praising the comfort the Judges enjoyed at the Castle, Durham. But he said there was some want of supellex [household furniture], *which they did not experience in other places. I asked him in what respects? He alluded more particularly, he said, to the want of plates and dishes so that when they had any number to dine with them they were obliged to be washed during the dinner… nor do I know exactly, with whom the responsibility of providing such things rests. If with the University, whose funds are not by any means what they ought to be, I beg leave to say, that I will gladly defray the expense of a neat, useful dinner and dessert set, with corresponding glass; the University undertaking to keep it up.* '*If this offer shall be at all acceptable, you will have the kindness to act upon it.'* (Thorp papers Vol.2, 320, 10 June 1838)

As a result, later in 1838 the University, acting on the Bishop's kindness, ordered a large service of crockery and glass, for the use of the High Court Judges when they lodged in the Castle during sittings of the Courts of Assize. The Maltby Service was manufactured by the Wedgwood factory: it bore the arms of Bishop Maltby and his initials [E D, for Edward Dunelm] surrounded by a border of signs of the zodiac (slightly oddly, perhaps, given that it was paid for by the Church – though a standard pattern probably kept the price down). The Bishop's arms were surmounted by the Palatine crest, a mitre encircled by a coronet, even though the previous bishop, Van Mildert,

A serving dish and plate from the Maltby service.

founder of the University, was technically the last of the 'Prince-Bishops'.

The Maltby service was used on special occasions in the College until the 1970s, but too little now remains for it to be usable and the finer surviving items are now confined to a display case on the Tunstal Gallery. Later additions to the service (presumably replacing breakages) carry different border designs: in some examples stars replace signs of the zodiac in an otherwise similar design; in others the border is a totally different surround of arches with reserved panels of flowers: it may be presumed that the expense of commissioning identical replacements was always too much for the College finances to bear.

Other services, of crockery and of silver and plate cutlery, were, of course, acquired for day-to-day use in the College. Much of this carried St. Cuthbert's Cross as its main design – and this was true even of more mundane items such as toilet sets (i.e. the water jugs and basins used for washing) and chamber pots.

Joe Bainbridge, The Castle Postman, by Clement Burlison, 1850.

there was, of course, no central heating, only dozens of open fires in the Kitchens, the Hall, the Common Rooms and individual sets of rooms. A small railway was constructed in the base of the keep for bringing in the coal – but the fuel still had to be hauled upstairs to each room, and fires had to be lit and maintained.

This in turn reminds us that, although the student body and the College community as a whole may not have been large, the College throughout its existence could not have functioned without a considerable staff of servants commanded by the Butler and the Housekeeper – kitchen staff, maids, handymen, porters, and so on – who were at least as much a part of the community as were the students and the dons. A number of these staff 'lived in' and were expected, for instance, to attend Chapel, where (at this date) Alfred Plummer (Master, 1874–1902) read instalments of his scripture commentaries instead of sermons.

[3] The second 50 years (1880s–1930s)

By the 1880s the University was well established and was gradually gaining in status. It was able to attract high-quality teaching staff, and some of its graduates, particularly in the field of divinity, were beginning to achieve a degree of eminence. University College and Hatfield Hall had been joined from 1871 by unattached (or non-collegiate) students, but even so the total number of students at Durham was still modest, topping 200 for the first time in 1882, the 50th anniversary year. At University College numbers had risen from 22 in 1873 to 50 in 1878, and reached a high of 79 in 1882.

Mention of such items prompts a mention of general living conditions within the Castle. These are hardly palatial today, but in the mid 19th century they were considerably more primitive. There was gas light in public areas from very early on, perhaps from the very beginning of the College; but there was no running water in rooms (there was a wash block on the south side of the Courtyard; otherwise water had to be carried upstairs); there was no modern sanitation inside the Castle – hence the need for chamber pots at night; and

The University therefore celebrated the anniversary in a mood of considerable optimism, awarding some forty honorary degrees, one of them a Doctorate of Divinity to John Cundill, the University's first student.

In University College the jubilee was marked by the installation of stained glass in the great north window of the Hall. Designed by C.E. Kempe, the window gives something of an heraldic history of the Castle, University and College: it displays the arms of the sees of York and Durham, and of the University; the arms of the Visitors (Bishops), Wardens and Masters of the University era; those of some of Durham's principal builders, Bishops Tunstal, Cosin, Crewe and Butler; and it carries images of Bishops Hatfield and Fox as well as St. George and St. Cuthbert.

This was only part of a major transformation of the Great Hall. The University had already, in the late 1840s, removed the rest of the stack of rooms that had once cut off the north end of the Hall (a room where the High Table now stands, known as the Black Parlour and used by the University as the Senior Common Room, and, above it, the Bishop's withdrawing room, latterly a lecture theatre). This made the Hall both bigger and lighter, for it could now once again benefit from light from the north. Indeed a new north window was installed in 1847, at the expense of the Warden, Charles Thorp (replacing a similar window, inserted by Hatfield, which been effectively redundant since the sub-division of the Hall) – and it was this new window which was now filled with stained glass.

Heating pipes had also just been installed around the Hall, powered from the room remaining beneath High Table (the dingy room once used for Choral Society concerts). The Hall's 17th-century panelling had been removed, and, again in the late 1840s, all but two of the windows had been extended downwards to their present length. The University now commissioned the architect C. Hodgson Fowler to design new panelling to run around the Hall as well as a screen, sideboard and gallery for the south end. These had all been installed by 1888.

The base of the north window in the Great Hall, showing St George and St Cuthbert flanked by Bishops Hatfield and Fox.

Restorations and alterations were also being carried out elsewhere in the Castle at the same time, most notably in the Tunstal Chapel. The Chapel had already been somewhat altered by the insertion of two large windows in the north wall in order to light the new stairway to the Keep. Efforts were now made to renovate the Chapel itself, and a new altar, wall-panelling and a richly-carved reredos, all in oak and again to designs by Hodgson Fowler, were in place by 1887. Since there was a chronic problem with damp in this part of the Castle (a problem still not entirely solved), other improvements included the replacement of the Chapel's wooden

Congregation (Graduation) ceremony in the Great Hall in 1895. The warden, Dean Lake, is shown presenting degrees, while seated to the right, one from left, is the Master, Alfred Plummer (1874–1902).

University College and the University of Durham

The east end of Tunstal's Chapel in 2007 (the front of the altar undergoing restoration at the time).

floor in stone, and the extension of the new heating system along the Tunstal Gallery from the Hall into the Chapel. The Chapel also acquired an organ, the choir organ of the old (late 17th-century) Father Smith instrument removed from the Cathedral in 1873, given to the College in 1879. Perhaps the principal mover behind many of the projects of this period was Walter Kercheval Hilton, the Bursar (1877-1913, and from 1883 also Censor). Bursars are not always popular, but this one was – and it is therefore fitting that the stained glass in the Chapel's south-east window is dedicated to his memory. The glass in the east window, installed in 1909, commemorates the Rev. H.A. White, Chaplain 1897-98. Both windows were again the work of C.E. Kempe's firm, though a generation later than Kempe's own design in the Great Hall.

In addition to these internal works, more serious structural problems were soon to become evident in the general fabric of the Castle, both in the north and west Ranges. These required very extensive buttressing and rebuilding work firstly in the first decade of the 20th century and then again in the late 1920s and 1930s (for which see chapter 5.3).

Meanwhile, the life of the College continued. Undergraduate numbers continued to give cause for concern, for after the record intake of 1882 they fell once more and were to fluctuate according to events for decades to come. Nonetheless, life for a Castle undergraduate at the turn of the 20th century seems to have been as pleasant as ever, if the reminiscences of C.F. Turnbull, a student in the late 1890s (*Castellum*, 1981), are anything to go by.

An 'extra' misericord, found 'in the old moat (c.1908) under Mr. Rushworth's premises in Saddler Street' and presented to the Chapel.

The pleasant but delapidated rooms (complete with deckchairs!) of CF Turnbull in the 1890s.

A change was soon to come, however, with the outbreak of the Great War in 1914 and the great Depression that followed it in the 1920s. War fever gripped the University along with the rest of the country in the years leading up to the outbreak of hostilities. A thriving Officers' Training Corps was led by officers drawn from the University's staff – among them W.D. Lowe (Bursar and Censor, 1913–21) and A.A. Macfarlane-Grieve (Master, 1939–53).

The Shooting Eight, 1914: their officers, WD Lowe and AA Macfarlane-Grieve, are seated left and right of the cup; Geoffrey Grimshaw is standing one from the right.

Many staff and students joined up at the outset of war, and others were subsequently called up – and collegiate life therefore virtually ceased. However, the College did not completely close down, and the *DUJ* (March

University College and the University of Durham

The organ and west end of Tunstal's Chapel.

Durham University Officer Training Corps. He volunteered and was killed in July 1916 at the Battle of the Somme. Even so, he was listed in the University Calendar for 1919–20 (which obviously took some time to catch up with events).

In the Castle there are two particular reminders of the Great War – in the Tunstal Chapel and in the College Library. In the Chapel, a new organ was commissioned from the well-known Durham firm of Harrison and Harrison as a memorial to members of College who died in the War. The new instrument, which deliberately retained the original front of pipes and a small portion of the old Father Smith organ, was completed and dedicated in 1925, and it is still in regular use today.

The Library, however, is a memorial of an individual: William Lowe, Bursar and Censor, returned to Durham after the war, and died in harness in 1921.

1916), speaking of the University as a whole, was able to comment that *'though so few men are in residence, we are proud to record that there is some College life'*.

Inevitably, a number of Castle students did not survive the War. Amongst them, to give just one example, was Geoffrey Harrison Grimshaw (1891–1916) who entered University College as an undergraduate in the Autumn of 1913. As well as being a member of the Durham University Hockey, Shooting and Boat clubs, he was an officer cadet in the

Portrait of Lt. Col. WD Lowe which hangs in the Lowe Memorial Library.

The 1944 College photograph; a mixture of formal and battle-dress.

He left his books to the College and from 1924 onwards they formed the nucleus of the Lowe Memorial Library, housed initially in Garden Stairs before being moved in 1959 to more spacious premises in the adjoining block, Hall Stairs.

Once the War was over, survivors came back to complete their studies, and others came up for the first time, and for a few years student numbers were once again quite healthy. By the later 1920s, however, the numbers were slumping again because of the Depression, and once again the University was obliged to take cost-saving measures. The Council of the Durham Colleges decided, amongst other things, to amalgamate the domestic administration of University College and Hatfield (the latter, after the War, finally styled a College rather than a mere Hall), and this seems to have had an effect:

'*Since that time [1926] students and staff of both colleges have taken their meals together in the Castle hall. This has effected a large reduction in cost, and has converted loss into a modest profit, thus making possible many improvements in the buildings and their equipment.*' (Edward Pace, in Whiting, 1937)

Even so, University College's undergraduate totals over the next few years fell back once again, to only 34 in 1928, and showed only a marginal rise, to 42, in what might be regarded as the centenary year, 1932. Nonetheless, by 1937 the dangerously unstable portions of the Castle had been rebuilt after a successful public appeal for funds, and the life of the College then continued without further major disruption – until the outbreak of the 2nd World War.

[4] The War years (1939–45)

From 1939 to 1953 the College had an old boy as its Master – A.A. Macfarlane-Grieve – a student (and briefly a tutor) just before the Great War, and Bursar (a post subsequently left vacant) from 1923. From 1940–49 he became Master of Hatfield as well, with Edward Pace as Vice-Master. As the University calendar reported:

'*For the duration of the war the two colleges are working in complete conjunction and a joint Governing Body has been established*'. [University Calendar, 1941–42]

Although the War naturally caused great disruption, both Colleges nonetheless remained lively, since they were home to a succession of cadets of the Durham University Air Squadron, undertaking Short Courses of some six months duration before being called up by the RAF. Designed specifically to turn out pilots, navigators and bomb-aimers for the Air Force, these courses had the additional benefit of helping to keep the Colleges open during the War years.

On each Course some one hundred Students in Arts or Sciences (spread between the two Colleges) completed their first year undergraduate studies within a truncated period (essentially two terms rather than three) while at the same time undertaking their military training. Formal photographs of the period thus show some men in gowns (which were worn for lectures) and others in uniform, depending on their day's activities. In spite of their full timetable and in spite of rationing and other war-time privations, Castle students of this period seem to have enjoyed themselves just as much as earlier and later generations, perhaps not least because the women's Colleges (St. Mary's, St. Hild's and Neville's Cross) also continued to operate throughout the War.

[5] A time to expand (1945–1980s)

The years after the War may have been a time of austerity for the nation as a whole, but for University College it was a time of rapid change and expansion. Many RAF personnel who had trained in College during the War came back to take or finish a degree, and thousands of other young men also applied to come to Durham: what had hitherto been a small, northern University became a medium-sized University with an intake from all over the country.

University College, a community of fewer (normally far fewer) than 100 students and staff for the first century of its existence, by the early 1950s suddenly had over 200 undergraduate and postgraduate students, and student numbers continued to increase through the 1950s and 60s (and, indeed, have done so right up to the present day). As a result, there was an immediate shortage of accomm-odation. Whereas students had previously occupied a pair of rooms (typically a relatively large sitting room and a smaller bedroom adjacent to it) the 'study-bedroom' now became the norm. In the Keep, by the mid-50s, each 'set' of rooms for a time housed three men, two of them sharing the larger room and the third enjoying single occupancy of the smaller one.

Various other houses on the peninsula were taken over by the College at various time: as well as Cosin's Hall these included several houses in Owengate (converted and partly rebuilt in 1962/3 and still in use); Abbey House, on the south-east corner of the Green (given up to the Theology Department in 1970); Bailey House (demolished in 1967 to make way for Bailey Court); and (across the river to the east) Parson's Field House, occupied by Castle students from 1967 until c.1975. In addition there were 'Durham Rooms', accommodation without board provided in various houses around the city (but charged, despite the inconvenience of coming into the Castle for meals, at the same rate as rooms in College).

The main addition, however, was Lumley Castle, leased by the University from the Earl of

Lumley Castle, c.1960.

Scarborough on a peppercorn rent from 1946 until 1969/70. Initially very dilapidated, this second Castle was rapidly converted to house another 75 students. However, the low rent notwithstanding, this was hardly the most economic or practical solution to the problem of lack of accommodation in Durham: there were now two castles to be staffed, and the Lumley students had to be bussed to Durham each day (taking their lunch or dinner in Durham Castle and other meals at Lumley). Nonetheless this sub-community was popular and operated successfully and with a fair degree of independence, under the direction of a Vice-Master.

Lumley and the unpopular 'Durham Rooms' were finally relinquished in 1970 when they were replaced by new purpose-built accommodation in Durham. This was Bailey Court, built on the site of the recently-demolished Bailey House and Museum Square, on the north-east side of the Green adjacent to Cosin's Hall and behind the Almshouses.

Dinner in the Great Hall at Lumley Castle.

It provided almost 120 study bedrooms in four four-storey blocks (imaginatively-named A, B, C and D) tucked neatly between Palace Green and North Bailey. The rooms are of reasonable size and appear bigger than they are since virtually all have large full-length windows.

By the late 1970s yet more rooms were required, and another new building, Moatside Court, part-way down Saddler Street, came into use in 1977, providing a further 127 single study-bedrooms – though the net gain was only 27 places since Parson's Field Court (some 50 rooms) was relinquished at the same time and 'A' stairs, Bailey Court (another 50 rooms), was

D-Block Bailey Court, which faces onto Palace Green.

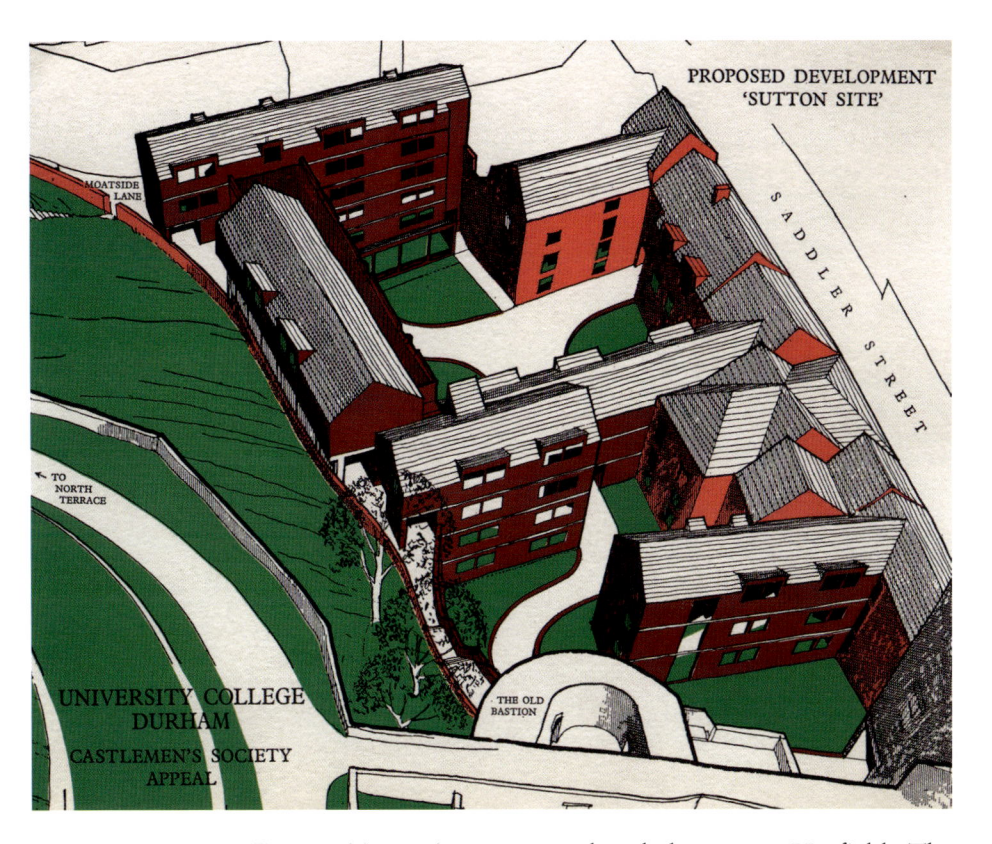

The cover of the appeal brochure detailing the proposed 'Sutton Site' development – which became Moatside Court.

handed over to Hatfield. The new Court comprised 'S' block, build around a small courtyard part-way down Saddler Street on the left (under the outer wall of the Castle, but with no communicating entranceway), as well as 'P', 'Q' and 'R' stairs just up-hill, between 'S' block and Owengate.

From the start Moatside was the least popular of the College's accommodation: the rooms were considerably smaller and darker than those of Bailey Court, and the walk to the Castle was longer (a projected path cutting up to the North Terrace never having been constructed). The author, as a 1st year undergraduate, was disappointed to be given a room in Moatside in 1979/80, then in its third year of use, and, despite periodic refurbishment, the accommodation is still hardly sought-after. On the plus side, however, Moatside is considerably closer to the Castle than outlying accommodation such as Parson's Field Court.

Freshmen of the period (myself included) found themselves allocated to Moatside (if they were not sharing in the Keep or elsewhere) and hoped to progress to Bailey Court, Owengate or the Castle in subsequent years (courtesy of a room ballot partially weighted in favour of those least fortunate first-time around). The new rooms did mean, however, that undergraduates could continue to be guaranteed accommodation 'in' College for all three years of their residence in Durham, a guarantee that, as the College expanded yet further, could not be given for very much longer.

An old postcard of the Courtyard at the turn of the 20th century; note the lack of a doorway to the Keep.

New oak furnishings were provided for the Chapel by Sir James Duff, Warden of the Durham Colleges (Vice-Chancellor in modern parlance), also as a War memorial. The only subsequent addition has been an oak 'Mouseman' lectern, one of a pair bought for the Castle and Hatfield by Chaplain Peter Brett (Joint Chaplain of University and Hatfield Colleges, 1966–72).

The Norman Undercroft to the Great Hall also received a makeover. Like the Norman Chapel it had been long neglected and it had been used by the University for storage and little else. A modern brick sub-

The new door to the Keep in the north east corner of the Courtyard.

The Undercroft in the 1980s.

Numerous other changes took place in the post-War decades, some of them welcome, others less so. Among the most welcome was the restoration of the Norman crypt Chapel, rededicated in 1951 as a memorial to the RAF personnel and other members of College who had lost their lives during the 2nd World War. This necessitated the removal of the stairway installed by the University at the east end of the chapel in 1840 to give access to the newly-restored Keep, and the opening up of a new entranceway to the Keep. This act of vandalism had been long regretted – (*'That it should have been made through the old Chapel is a grievous mistake, which cannot now be corrected'*, said the 1900 edition of the Castle guidebook) – and it was now finally undone.

The Norman Chapel in the 1840s, drawn by RW Billings, complete with stairs to the Keep.

The restored Chapel.

division down the centre of the Undercroft was removed in 1961, and the single room that resulted became the Junior Common Room and, eventually, the College Bar. The latter was officially licensed from the mid-1970s; but beer and other beverages had been previously been available in College at meal times as in any other 'private house' (though at a price that appeared later on the termly 'battels' bill).

The social revolution that swept the country in the 1960s was naturally reflected in other changes in College. With the lowering of the national Age of Majority from 21 years to 18, there was no longer any real necessity for the dons to act 'in loco parentis' to the students, and, partly as a result, the student body was gradually allowed more power and influence within the University as well as more freedom of action within College.

There was a gradual relaxation of the curfew hour: the gates, originally locked at 10 pm and later at 11, were from 1961 closed only at midnight; and in the late 60s the restrictions were effectively removed when residents were issued with keys to the postern gate.

There was a general increase in student representation on committees, including the Governing Body of University College, and the students were encouraged to take charge of various aspects of their life in College. Not the least important of these to the students themselves was that from the mid-1960s the JCR had, in term, complete control of the running of the Undercroft Bar.

Several less popular moves came in the mid-70s, in particular the abolition in 1976 of the majority of the served formal meals enjoyed in Hall by the students since the foundation of the College. The kitchens (being designed, after all, to cater for the Bishops' banquets) were well able to cope with increasing numbers, but there was a limit to how many could be seated in Hall, and there were also, as ever, financial considerations. Nightly formal meals for the undergraduates vanished – Tuesday and Thursday evenings and Sunday lunch remained – to be replaced by 'informal' meals collected in the recently-constructed Servery (formed in the 50s from what had until then been the silver pantry and the staff dining room) to the west of the Hall. Incidentally, new servants' quarters had also been constructed in the 50s on two floors below the Servery, since a number of College servants still 'lived in' even at this date.

The College had to wait until the late 1980s, however, for the most noticeable, and arguably the most important change so far – the admission of women to first the Senior Common Room and then also to the Junior Common Room.

[6] A mixed and modern college (1987–2004)

1981 marked the centenary of the University's decision to admit women to the University's courses, though it was the 1890s before the decision was put into practice. By the 1980s the University had long boasted several successful women's colleges, such as St. Mary's and St. Aidan's, as well as mixed colleges such as Collingwood and all-male colleges such as Castle and Hatfield.

The students of University College were hardly deprived of female society: Castlemen had long felt welcome in the bars of Mary's, Aidan's and elsewhere, and there was no segregation in the lecture rooms, academic departments, or social activities of the University. Even so, many felt it unfair to deny women the opportunity of attending what Castlemen at least still regarded as the University's foremost College, and falling application rates made it clear that potential students

The Freshers photo, 1987 – the first to include ladies.

As a result University College took the decision (not without some opposition) to open the SCR to women members, and shortly afterwards the students also voted narrowly in favour of 'going mixed'. This was fortuitous (since the decision had already been taken by the College authorities) and also remarkable in that the students of other colleges, notably Hatfield and St. Mary's, were strongly opposed to the idea. In Autumn 1987 the first Castlewomen were admitted, and in 1993 the students elected their first female Senior Man, Anna Cope (for the students decided, bizarrely, to retain the title regardless of the sex of the office holder). were in any case increasingly opting for mixed, rather than single-sex, colleges.

Applications to the College immediately soared. There are now consistently well over 2000 applications annually for about 180 places and (although a few people regretted the passing of old ways and traditions) in the opinion of most the College became at a stroke a more vibrant and enjoyable place in which to live and work. At present, quite by chance, there is an exact 50/50 split between the sexes in University College.

I seem to remember making three, slightly tongue-in-cheek, predictions when the College went mixed: that the decibel level at breakfast would rise; that the population of College would go down (since some girl-friends might now live in officially!); and that the standard of food would rise (because the women would either have the good sense to complain or would vote with their feet by staying away). All, I think, have been borne out, though the quality of the food is always an issue and is currently being addressed once again (this time through the appointment of an 'executive chef').

Going mixed required a few changes, of course, not least to the accommodation. Initially the women were housed on particular corridors in Bailey Court and elsewhere while arrangements could be made to provide a little more privacy in shower blocks and so on; but once the changes had been made, the College became fully mixed. Night-time security also became more of an issue, since it was not only considered important for the women to feel safe in College but also that they actually *were* safe. Partly for this reason, the way in which the Castle Lodge operated was altered after the retirement of Cicely Shaw (whose family had lived in the Gatehouse for half a century): it is now manned 24-hours a day rather than closing at midnight.

It was also a matter of some concern to the College authorities that many individuals failed to lock their rooms at night, since a number of the accommodation blocks had hitherto rarely been locked at night – and up to that time, indeed, the outer doors of Bailey Court actually had no locks at all. The obvious solution, however, to install locks and use them, was not universally popular with the students, for this placed something of a restriction on individual liberty, i.e. friends could not visit so easily with a locked outer door in the way.

The latter objection largely vanished with the coming of the mobile phone, a change that has revolutionised Durham and national society alike: no longer do students queue for the public telephones to communicate with their parents; no longer do they rely on the University's internal mail system to

The procession leaves the Castle on the way to the Matriculation Ceremony in the Cathedral, October 2006.

communicate with other Colleges; and no longer do they gain entry to each other's blocks (and disturb others) by shouting up to their friends.

Another national revolution, the spread of computer technology, has also had its effects, some so obvious there no need to mention them, others less so. It appears, for instance, to have had an effect on the patterns of work and play in College. In the 70s and 80s, when a significant percentage of students began to be delivered by car and thus could bring with them large quantities of luggage, no self-respecting undergraduate would be without the stereo system or ghetto-blaster. Music could be then be played in a student's room at a volume hitherto un-heard, and many held parties in their own accommodation blocks rather than necessarily always going out to pubs or discos. College was often, therefore, a rather noisy place, even when ruthlessly policed by the resident dons.

This trend appears to have reversed somewhat in the internet age: many students still bring a (more modestly-sized) music system, but many, if not most, now also have a laptop computer. Thus – though I fear this may be my age speaking – it appears that students now do more work in their study-bedrooms than once they did. There is, apparently, less need to go to the library or computer rooms (partly because one of the major achievements of the 21st century in College has been the cabling for internet access of every student's room), but they have reverted to going out to socialize.

Various College traditions have been modified in concert with the times: gowns, for instance, have become an increasingly rare sight, largely reserved for the most important University events (such as Matriculation and Congregation, that is admission and graduation), Chapel, and formal meals. By the late 1980s student attendance at formal meals had become very sparse, and the formal Sunday lunch was abolished as an economy measure, with hardly a whisper of protest. Modern Castle students, however, obviously have a sneaking liking for tradition and formality (indeed I suspect many would admit that they applied to University College specifically in order to live in a Castle), and in recent years Tuesday and Thursday formal dinners have become immensely popular once more, so much so that students have to 'sign in' at the lodge in order to secure a place – and there is virtually always a waiting list.

The College's intake is increasingly diverse: all the academic departments are represented in College, for the University assigns a quota for each subject to which the College has to adhere fairly rigidly, a deliberate mixing of subjects which is extremely beneficial both to the College community and to the way in which its members integrate into the wider University community. In

Congregation, 1982: the scene in the Courtyard after a ceremony in the Great Hall.

(1979–83) one of the great attractions of Castle, and indeed of Durham University generally, was the guarantee of accommodation for all three years of your undergraduate career. Virtually everybody lived in, with the exception of a dozen or so people granted special permission to move out in their final year.

Twenty five years later, the College has doubled in size and it can no longer make that guarantee, and virtually all undergraduates are required to live out in their second year. Indeed, such is the pressure of numbers that a few 'livers in' have recently had to be housed in rented houses elsewhere in the town (a modern version of 'Durham Rooms'), while fully one third of the student population of the College now lives 'out' in self-catering accommodation. Similarly, in my day there was also a strong likelihood of being able to continue to 'live in' as a postgraduate, if that is what suited you (and it suited me). Now, because of the huge number of undergraduates, we have only a small number of resident postgraduates.

There are now, therefore, gaps in the College between the 1st- and 3rd-year undergraduates, and between the JCR and the SCR. These gaps, once filled by the 2nd-years and the MCR, now need to be deliberately bridged if they are not to have a detrimental effect on the community. Various social events such as 'livers out formals' and a College Feast have been instituted, as well as changes to the College's Tutorial system; and the undergraduate body operates an admirable 'mentoring' scheme to help the 1st years (the 'freshers') settle in.

One of the things which visitors to the University frequently ask is for a definition of the difference between a college and a hall of residence. It is not easy to come up with a simple answer, and, perhaps because of this, there is an increasing tendency (even, it must be said, amongst some of the academic and administrative staff of this University) to assume that

Marshalling before Congregation in the Great Hall, 1998. (The recent expansion of the University means that Congregation ceremonies now take place in the Cathedral.)

terms of school background, in October 2004 the new intake included 31% from Comprehensive schools; 9% from Grammar schools; 15% from Further Education or 6th-Form Colleges; and 41% from the Independent sector. Unfortunately that intake was still predominantly southern and middle class: only about 7 or 8 per cent of admissions at present come from the north-east, a figure which both the University and College authorities would like to see rise, not least so that the University is more obviously a part of the wider community and the people of Co. Durham can regard Durham Castle and University College as their own.

The rapid expansion of the University in recent decades, at least in part in response to government targets, has placed some strain on the College system. When I was a student

University College and the University of Durham

Congregation, 1998: the staff procession.

there is no real difference between the two. Those of us who have been lucky enough to live and work in a college environment know that nothing could be further from the truth.

At Oxford or Cambridge there is an obvious difference to which one can point: a large amount of teaching is carried out in individual colleges and they can thus be readily seen as separate academic entities within the overall umbrella of their respective Universities. However, at Durham there is not the money to maintain such a system, and teaching and research takes place, as it has always done here, within the framework of the academic departments. Even tutorials take place elsewhere, for the College's resident dons, of whom there are now very few, nearly all have offices more suitable for the purpose in their respective departments.

Colleges at Durham lack any separate corporate status and also lack the property, income and patronage enjoyed by Oxbridge colleges. Accordingly, they exercise relatively little managerial or financial autonomy within the University. Increasingly (for this is something that has changed quite rapidly in recent years), managerial and organizational decisions are taken at University rather than College level, so that the Master of University College is much less powerful than he once was, and the Governing Body, now known as the College Council, is similarly reduced in status. In addition, since budgets are also set centrally, the role of the College Bursar has been effectively downgraded. Thus, from this perspective, the College is clearly less important than it was a generation or so ago.

Nonetheless, the Colleges at Durham still have an important part to play, not least in the admission of students, the maintenance of discipline and the provision of pastoral care. They give the University a very distinctive flavour, a flavour which derives, I think, first and foremost, from the sense of community that a College provides. In my opinion it is this that most clearly marks the difference between a college and a mere hall of residence, and there can be no doubt that the sense of community is alive and well in University College, Durham.

Congregation, 1998: the Chancellor, Sir Peter Ustinov, follows the procession into the Great Hall.

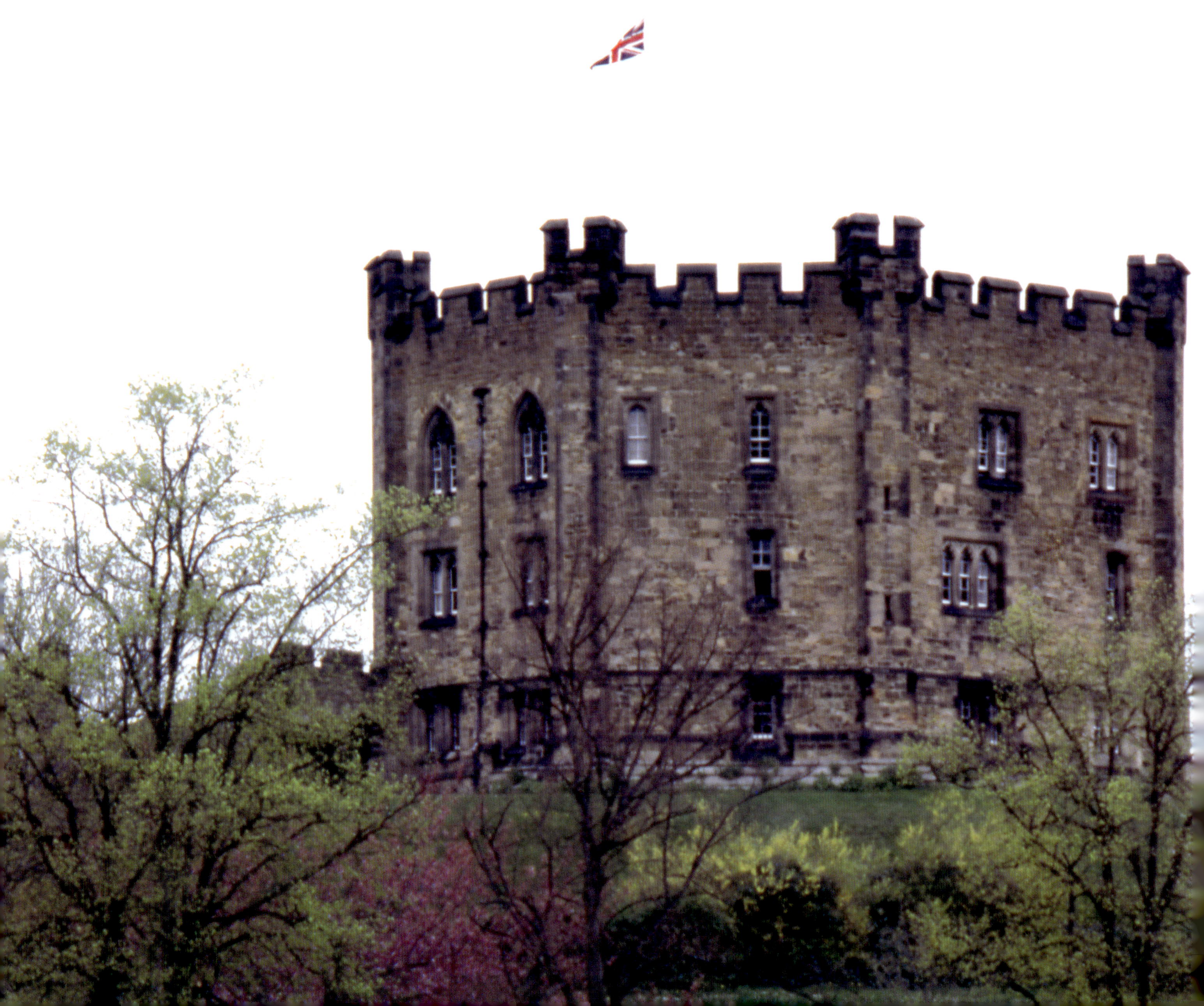

Chapter Five

Durham Castle in the 21st Century

[1] A brief tour of the Castle and College

The Castle is approached from the south along a driveway which follows the line of the former Barbican and crosses the line of the old dry moat to reach the Gatehouse. The stone slab and cobble surface is these days rather uneven, owing to the passage of large modern vehicles. Both the driveway and the building itself are illuminated at night by floodlights of a warm yellow colour (first installed *c.*1971), contrasting with the colder white which lights the Cathedral.

The Gatehouse on the Norman Castle, already substantially altered by Tunstal and Cosin, was rebuilt at the end of the 18th century by James Wyatt for Bishop Barrington and extensively refurbished in 1991 after the retirement of the last resident gatekeeper. It now houses a Porter's Lodge and en-suite student rooms. The ground floor room on the eastern side of the arch at present provides the Castle's only 'wheelchair friendly' accommodation (since there are stairs virtually everywhere else).

Beyond the Gatehouse is the Courtyard, originally the Inner Bailey of the Norman Castle. Today it presents a peaceful scene, with a large circular lawn in its centre surrounded by a surfaced turning circle. Vehicles may be allowed beyond the Gatehouse at the discretion of the Porter, but stringent modern fire regulations restrict the number to a maximum of six at any given time and access is therefore normally granted only for the purpose of loading or unloading. The old well in the Courtyard is covered over by tarmac (though it was rediscovered in 1904 and found to be over 100 feet in depth, with the main supply of water coming in about 70 feet down); and the fountain set into the east wall is now merely a feature amongst the flower beds.

The eastern side of the Courtyard is still dominated by the Keep, though it is not the original or even Hatfield's replacement but Anthony Salvin's Gothic-style re-building of 1840, expressly designed to provide student accommodation. In term-time it now houses about 60 students, in a mixture of single and twin rooms, while a further dozen students live in the Junction, the name now given to rooms opening off the stairway leading to the Keep (and also part of Salvin's rebuild).

Conditions are much more cramped than they were in the 19th century, when each student was afforded a pair of rooms, comprising a large sitting room and a smaller bedroom next door. Coal fires have long since been replaced by radiators (the latter themselves now of rather antiquated design) so the little tunnel and railway that allowed coal to be wheeled into the base of the Keep have now been sealed off (to the disappointment of old Castlemen who once used to take pleasure in using that illicit entrance to the Castle).

The Keep's current entrance is a doorway inserted in 1951/2 in the north-east corner of the Courtyard below the Tunstal Chapel. This provided more convenient access to both the Junction and Keep which prior to that had been reached by a stairway through the Norman Chapel.

On the left immediately inside this modern doorway is a panelled room (the lower part of Tunstal's Chapel range) previously accessible only through a door set in one of the (now blocked) archways inserted by Tunstal in the south wall of the Norman Chapel. This room was the Junior Common Room (the JCR) for over a century until, in the 1960s, with student numbers on the increase, the Undercroft was renovated and took over that function; in the 1970s and 80s it was the College's Television Room; and it has now become the Middle Common Room, the preserve of the postgraduate students. This is a particularly important development since it once again gives the postgraduates a place of their own within the Castle: from 1960 postgraduate 'Thorp Club' briefly occupied a room on Hall Stairs before being relocated off the Norman Gallery (for the remainder of the 1960s and the early 1970s); and, in the early 1980s, the postgraduates were allocated in a room in Owengate – but for a while they had no base in College.

The Norman Range and the work of Bishop Tunstal dominate the north side of the Courtyard just as they did in the 16th century. Tunstal's Chapel, in the north-east corner of the Courtyard, is in frequent use during term, the main services being at 6 pm on a Thursday, before Formal Dinner, and at 11am on Sunday. The College has a resident Chaplain

The Clock – newly restored in 2006.

(technically half-time since he or she also holds the Solway Research Fellowship) and a well-regarded College Choir made up of students and senior members of the College community.

The Bell-Tower has a single bell (dating from 1705) which can be rung from the bottom of the stair that leads from the Courtyard to the Chapel. It is now also the Clock-Tower. A clock had been mounted in the tower above the Gatehouse by Bishop Cosin in the 1660s; that was removed by Wyatt in the late 18th century and replaced at a lower level (where there is now a circular window). In the early days of the University, however, sometime between 1838 and 1844, this clock, or a new one, was installed in the bell-tower in the Courtyard – but by 1882 it had ceased to function and was taken down. The Courtyard then lacked a timepiece for more than half a century until the present electrically-driven mechanism was installed in 1950 as a war memorial. The new clock retained the 19th-century wooden clock-face, but it was too worn to be refurbished and was therefore overlain by a copper disc with painted gold numerals. Unfortunately, by late 2005 the wood had warped so far that it prevented the hands of the clock from turning – and it therefore had to be replaced.

Tunstal's Gallery, designed to link the Great Hall and his Chapel, still performs that function for students and staff as well as for tourists taking the guided tour. 19th-century prints show undergraduates relaxing on benches on the Gallery, but in recent years student access has been more restricted and the Gallery is most often used for receptions prior to meals in the Senate Suite or the Great Hall. Display cases lining the walls house china and military equipment, part of the permanent exhibition of the Museum's collections.

Below the Gallery is another room of similar size, the Lower Tunstal Gallery. From the outset it may have been partitioned into several smaller rooms (accessed via additional small doorways, opening directly into the Courtyard). These rooms were used by tutors in the early years of the University but by *circa* 1900 the dividing walls had been removed to create a single Gallery. The main entrance is via a large doorway directly below the window in the main Tunstal Gallery that frames the Norman Arch (a doorway enlarged by the University in *circa* 1840 as the entranceway to the Keep). Often used principally as a storeroom in recent decades, the Lower Gallery has now become, during vacations, the Hotel and Conference Reception area even though it is not exactly ideally placed to perform this function, being on the far side of the Courtyard from the Gatehouse.

To the west of the Galleries, in the north-west corner of the Courtyard is the large tower built by Bishop

Cosin to house the Black Stairs. The Stairs are still in daily use, though a precautionary limit of 40 is placed on the size of guided tours specifically in order not to overload the ancient staircase. As one climbs there is a rather alarming list to starboard, but all movement seems to have been arrested very early on by the supporting upright timbers added to what was originally a flying staircase. Again, student access to this part of the Castle is restricted, with the Norman Gallery normally being gained via the Norman Spiral Stair at the eastern end of the Gallery rather than via the Black Stairs at the west end.

The Spiral Stair (which previously gave access to the Norman Chapel from above until diverted in c.1840) links the Norman Gallery with the eastern end of the Lower Tunstal Gallery and the Courtyard. It also gives access to the organ loft though no longer to the Tunstal Chapel itself, for an

The Tunstal Chapel with the bell-tower and galleries beyond it.

earlier doorway in the Chapel's lobby is now blocked. It also allows access (via a little hatch normally used only by those looking to service the heating system) to a large void, the remains of earlier rooms, extending right under the Senate Suite and down behind the Lower Tunstal Gallery.

Also at the base of the Spiral Stair lies the Norman Chapel, probably the oldest surviving part of the Castle. Although a beautiful little building retaining some remarkable early sculpture on the capitals of its columns, it was so little regarded in the early years of the University that a staircase was constructed through its east wall to provide access to the rebuilt Keep (the Chapel first being entered via a tunnel driven through from the Lower Tunstal Gallery) – but the staircase was blocked up and the Chapel restored in the early 1950s when the present entranceway to the Keep was opened up under Tunstal's Chapel.

The Chapel was rededicated in 1951, partly as a war memorial to those members of College who lost their lives during the 2nd World War. It is now in regular use once more – and not just by Anglicans but also by various other Christian denominations as well. A memorial book on the Tunstal Gallery gives the names of the Castlemen, members of the RAF, Home Guard and other services, who lost their lives during the War, and also records the names of those who have died in subsequent engagements such as the Falklands.

The Norman Gallery, and most of the rooms off it, are occupied by students in term-time, as they have been throughout the College's history. The Gallery is much valued by the student body and, although the Gallery rooms are not palatial and the only bathroom is part-way down the Spiral Stairs, for some decades now it has largely been the 'student

The Norman Gallery in the 1840s, by RW Billings.

Durham Castle in the 21st Century

The rooms at the eastern end of the Gallery form what was once the College Censor's set. This is now divided in two: the western half is the room occupied from 1962/3 by the Thorp Club (a postgraduate club, forerunner of the MCR), but it is now a study-bedroom occupied by two undergraduates in term and is further transformed into a 'family room' in the vacations; the other half is now one of a handful of 'don's sets' dotted around the Castle (this one until recently occupied by the author). The living room of this particular set blocks off what, for part of the University's history, must have been rather a convenient corridor between the newly-constructed Junction and Keep and the Norman Range: now, as in the Norman period, it is only possible to pass between the two areas by descending to Courtyard level.

At the western end of the Gallery there is a fascinating little room now occupied by the JCR Secretary which looks (from its high pointed ceiling) as though it were once a small oratory, perhaps the Bishop's private chapel. It is built into the north-west corner tower, which is thought to be an addition to le Puiset's building, made in the latter years of the reign of King John at a time when the bishopric was vacant (1209–16). In the days when students enjoyed a pair of rooms the 'oratory' became a sitting room: the accompanying bed-room, now the JCR office, was across the Gallery and just through doors leading to the Black Stairs.

Decayed stonework (the remains of a garderobe tower) and the windows of the Norman Gallery rooms, viewed from the North Terrace.

executive', the Senior Man and other elected officials of the JCR, who have lived there. The Gallery itself has recently become a much brighter place, with the addition of five large chandeliers intended to match the grander style of lighting found elsewhere in the north range.

Most of the rooms on the Gallery, bedrooms originally inserted in the time of Crewe or thereabouts, were remodelled in the 1970s. 19th-century students had occupied a pair of rooms (as they did in the Keep), but increasing student numbers and the consequent constraints on space led to the alteration and partitioning of once much more spacious accommodation.

The JCR Secretary's room at the west end of the Norman Gallery.

Passing down the Stairs, the first rooms to be encountered are the Bishop's Suite and the Chaplain's office, on the level below the Norman Gallery. The Suite, which is hung with 17th-century tapestries and furnished with some of the best material in the Castle's collections, is so called because these were the rooms reserved for the Bishop's use when the rest of the building was handed over to the University in 1837 – and the Bishop still retains the right to use them. Today, however, the Suite is commercially let as a rather grand bedroom suite, and is frequently occupied by wedding couples following their reception in the Great Hall.

Adjacent to the Suite is a little room that once connected to it and was either a dressing room and/or was occupied by a valet. Today it is the Chaplain's office. It, and the small JCR

The entranceway to the 'Upper Norman Gallery' from the Junction Roof.

Above the Norman Gallery lies one of the Castle's better-kept secrets, another gallery running the full length of the Norman range. It can be accessed only from a door (converted from a 16th-century window) on the Junction roof, and is lit only by a tall 14th-century window at its west end (visible from Framwellgate Bridge). Despite the (very expensive) pipe-dream of converting this huge space to provide further accommodation, at present it houses water tanks and little else.

At the same level but at the top of the Black Stairs is a very pleasant pair of rooms, known as the "Crow's Nest". They were once a bedroom and sitting room, but modern fire regulations dictate that they can no longer be used for living purposes. Accordingly they now provide a workroom and archive and picture store for the Curator as well as much-needed storage space for the Housekeeper.

The interior of the Upper Gallery – ripe for conversion!

The spiral ends today on the level below (though another redundant passage can be traced down to ground level one floor further down). It led into a passage now blocked to the north by the south wall of the Chaplain's Suite, a passage that once led into the rooms at the west end of le Puiset's Lower Hall.

The Chaplain's Suite has no current connection with the Chaplain, even though its name suggests that at one time it did. In the 1830s the Bishop proposed to retain it for the use of his servants when he was in residence in the Bishop's Suite immediately above. At that date it was described as the 'Still Room' (perhaps not actually used for distilling liquor but as a pantry/storeroom).

The Chaplain's Suite is now also commercially let, and, after the Bishop's Suite, is the most sought-after accommodation in the Castle. At some stage in the mid-19th century it was converted into two rooms with separate access doors from the SCR lobby/anteroom. The two rooms cannot, however, be let separately because only the northern room has a bathroom (built over the old garderobe, the primitive medieval equivalent of the toilet).

Across the anteroom from the Suite, and up a short stairway, lies the Senior Common Room, once the Bishop's Dining Room. It is the largest and most imposing of the State Rooms inserted into the shell of the Norman range. The walls are hung with oil paintings from the Castle's collections and it retains its 'Strawberry Hill Gothic' ceiling. The Senior Common Room is reserved for the (almost) exclusive use of the senior members of the College, who guard this privilege jealously. The SCR now has around 400 members, drawn from throughout the University and the wider community, though perhaps only about 60 might be regarded as 'regulars'.

office above it (immediately outside the Norman Gallery), occupy part of the line of the old spiral staircase rendered redundant when the Black Stairs were built – and a small part of the spiral survives below the Chaplain's floor.

The Bishop's Suite Bedroom.

The SCR anteroom therefore allows access to both the Chaplain's Suite and the SCR. It opens off the west end of the Tunstal Gallery and also leads to the North Terrace, via a large door inserted in its north wall. The room was once part of the accommodation taken over by the Judges of Assize during their thrice-yearly visits: the Judges occupied the main bedrooms in the Bishop's Suite (the Senior Judge's apartment) and the Senate Suite; their staff slept in the Chaplain's Suite; and the anteroom was converted into a staff sitting room using temporary panels set into grooves in the floor. Currently the anteroom sees a variety of uses: as a breakfast room (for guests in the Chaplain's Suite); as a convenient location for College Tutors' to meet and entertain their student charges; and, since the installation of a 'Baby Grand' piano, as a music practice room.

To the east of the SCR, down a short flight of stairs, there is a small kitchen where meals were prepared for the Judges – and even though the latter ceased staying in the Castle in 1971, the room is still known as the Judges' Kitchen. It is now largely used as a staging post between the main kitchens and the Senate Suite when functions are held in that Suite.

The Senate Suite, further east again, is also named for an earlier function, since the University Senate used to meet in the main room in the 19th century. The anteroom to the Suite and the Octagon Room on its west side are, like the SCR, built into the old Norman range, while the main Senate Room occupies the site of what was probably the Castle's chapel between the 12th and 16th centuries. The set of rooms was designed as the Bishop's Withdrawing and Bedroom Suite and is probably an early 18th-century remodelling of older rooms. The main room retains its set of 17th-century tapestries, as well as an elaborate 17th-century overmantel, while the other rooms house more of the Castle's collection of oils and watercolours. Latterly the Suite has been used as a series of function rooms, being hired out for meetings, conferences, drinks receptions and dinner parties. Weddings receptions for relatively small numbers (up to 50 guests) are often staged in the Senate Suite rather than in the Great Hall.

Beyond the Senate Room itself, the Bishop's Bedroom has been converted into another meeting room, currently known as the Green Room. If the meeting is dull, there is a ready source of entertainment to hand: the Green Room's (pink!) walls are hung with a number of examples of the sketches of Cuthbert Bede, illustrating life in Durham in the mid-19th century.

The Senate Suite is accessed from the Tunstal Gallery via the Norman Arch, the magnificent example of late Norman (Romanesque) architecture that once framed the main entrance to Bishop le Piuset's 12th-century hall. Originally approached via a flight of steps from the Castle Courtyard (since it is on 1st-floor level) and probably protected by a canopy (since it is so well preserved), it has suffered a chequered history. Obviously down-graded in importance after the building of Tunstal's Gallery in front of it in the 16th century, the opening was at one time reduced to a small window only (the hinges are still visible); but it was rediscovered and opened up once more in the late 18th century. Now carefully restored, it is one of the main focal points of the guided tour.

Passing back along the Tunstal Gallery and half a turn further down the Black Stairs one comes to the Great Hall, one of the main focal points of College life. This has been, since the late 1830s, the dining hall of the College, where residents take their meals throughout the University term. There have been changes, however: in 1970, for the benefit of ladies, chairs (modelled on those purchased for the Library a decade earlier) replaced the old benches; and, where once all meals would

Concert in the Great Hall, *Illustrated London News*, 22 March 1851.

have been served at table, there are now, for the undergraduates, only two 'formal' meals per week, on Tuesday and Thursday evenings (though the SCR preserve memories of an earlier era by dining formally every week day on the high table at the north end of the hall).

'Formal' meals are 'waitress-served', those present wear gowns and the meal is begun with a spoken grace. The rest of the meals are termed 'informal': originally this still meant a served meal, but one where the formalities were dispensed with; but since the mid-1970s 'informals' have also been 'self-service', with the students queuing up in the Screens Passage to collect their meals as they pass through the modern Servery into the Hall.

During the vacations the Hall is almost equally busy, with the College staff catering for hotel and bed-and-breakfast guests as well as frequent wedding receptions and other grand meals. At various times of the year plays and concerts are performed in the Hall (as they have been since the 1830s), but the University Congregation ceremonies, held there since 1837, have since Summer 2002 taken place in the Cathedral because of the ever-increasing numbers of students.

Although built in the 13th and 14th centuries for Bishops Bek and Hatfield (and variously known over the years as Bek's Hall, Hatfield's Hall, the White Hall and now the Great Hall), the interior of the Hall very much reflects the years of occupation by the University. Of particular note is the great north window with its stained glass by Kempe; while the panelling, the furniture, many of the paintings and the downward extension of some of the windows also date to the 19th or 20th centuries.

While still a very impressive hall, being some 45 feet high, 35 feet wide and over 100 feet long, the Great Hall was about a third longer again until shortened by Bishop Fox in the 1490s (the great fireplace would originally have been in the middle of the west wall rather than towards one end). The southern end of the Hall is now occupied by the Screens Passage, the College Library and Hall Stairs.

The Screens Passage and the Fonteyn doors. The diagonally-laid slabs in the foreground (representing Cosin's coat of arms) were moved from the centre of the Great Hall in c.1930 when the Hall floor of 1663 was replaced in wood. Two doors (one barely visible on the right) gave access to Fox's apartments but are now sealed to provide a fire screen between the Hall and the adjacent Hall Stairs accommodation.

The Screens Passage, which passes along the back of the Hall between the Castle's main entrance (framed since the 1660s by Bishop Cosin's porch) and the Buttery, provides a very welcome wind break between the Hall and the outside world.

It contains one of the most recent modifications to the Castle, the Fonteyn Doors, named in memory of Dame Margot Fonteyn, onetime Chancellor of the University. They, in effect, double the layer of defences against the elements provided by the Screens Passage, and the Hall has been a noticeably warmer place since their installation in AD 2000.

The Buttery is no longer much used for its traditional purpose, the storage of food and wine, for food storage rooms are now situated on the other side of the Kitchen, beneath Garden Stairs, and the wine cellars are now beneath the Servery. It is, however, still one of the main hubs of daily activity in College: off this enclosed and covered courtyard may be found not only the Kitchen but also the Housekeeping and Catering Offices and, to the north, the Servery.

The Kitchen continues to provide meals for all residents in term time and for the various guests and functions throughout the year. The Kitchen fireplaces, brickwork, ceiling (of chestnut wood) and the east and west windows as well as most of the woodwork in the Buttery remain substantially unchanged since the time of Bishop Fox, 500 years ago. The equipment used today is obviously different – for the three medieval fireplaces are no longer in use and the ancient wooden tables on which food was prepared for so long have been banished to other parts of the Castle – but the essential function of this part of the Castle has probably not changed in over 900 years. Indeed the remains of what are probably the Castle's earliest ovens and brew house are still preserved amongst the modern water pipes immediately below the present Kitchen.

The doors between the Screens Passage and Buttery, the woodwork re-used from the 17th-century organ screen in the Cathedral.

The Buttery and Kitchen, by JR Brown (d.1913). These images probably date from the late 19th century.

Beneath the Great Hall, accessible from two doors in the Courtyard and a stairway from next to the Buttery, is the Norman Undercroft, one of the earliest surviving parts of the Norman Castle, for this is the Undercroft to the original West Hall. It is, without doubt, the other great focal point of College (and, Castlemen would say, University) life – for the Undercroft is now the Bar, the students' 'Undie', a busy and lively place virtually every night in term. The Bar is also open in the vacation, for the benefit of guests.

Beyond the Undercroft to the north lies the West Courtyard Room, built in the 1980s, over a previously-open courtyard, as a separate Junior Common Room (for until then the Undercroft had performed that function as well). Very recently a further series of smaller Common Rooms, accessed from the West Courtyard Room, has been manufactured immediately west of the Undercroft, reusing what were once servants' rooms – for the College has had no resident serving staff for some years now (the last being John Atkin, who moved out in 1983).

The new rooms are popular with the students and are also useful as conference rooms during the vacations. The money for much of this work (and for remodelling the toilet block next door) came from the University College, Durham Trust, largely thanks to the efforts and generosity of old Castlemen.

Moneys raised by the Trust also allowed the downward extension of the College Library in the mid 1990s to encompass what had hitherto been a wine cellar. The Library therefore now occupies much of three floors of Hall Stairs, the block of rooms constructed in the late 15th century in the south end of the Great Hall. When transferred from its original home in Garden Stairs, the Lowe Library was housed on the ground floor only, but a decade later (*c*.1970) it expanded into the room above (reached from below by a spiral staircase), a room hitherto used as a common room by 'livers out', the occupants of the 'Durham Rooms' mentioned above.

Despite periodic proposals to do away with such libraries (on the grounds that they merely duplicate the holdings of the University Library), the Lowe Library is generally held to be an extremely useful feature of University College and in the summer term in particular it is heavily used. Indeed such is the demand for books and for work space that the Minstrels' Gallery, at the south end of the present Great Hall, a space otherwise little used in modern times other than for storage, has recently been converted into additional library space. This has been possible thanks to a generous donation by Dr. Ian Doyle (commemorating more than half a century as a member of the College) and further funds from the Trust.

Much of the remainder of the Castle is given over to accommodation. The Keep has already been mentioned, and Hall Stairs. In the latter the remaining rooms comprise a don's set (above the Library) where, of late, visiting Fellows are often accommodated; two Computer Rooms; and a handful of student study-bedrooms.

It may be that the Computer Rooms, established a decade or so by popular demand, will become redundant in years to come, now that the students' own rooms are cabled for internet access.

South of Hall Stairs, in the south-west corner of the Courtyard, is Garden Stairs, which contains some of the more sought-after rooms in the Castle. Until the early 1990s this block housed the College Offices, but these were transferred to the top floor of a new building in the Fellows' Garden in 1992, allowing the Garden Stairs rooms to be converted into en-suite accommodation (of which, because of Planning restrictions, the Castle has very little).

The downward extension of the College Library. Note on the right-hand side the ancient column of a style very similar to those in the Norman Chapel, but here re-used upside down.

The Fellows Garden building technically lies outside the Castle, since it is outside the walls of the old Inner Bailey astride the line of the old dry moat, but it is entered via the Porter's Lodge in the west side of the Gatehouse. It is a two-storey building, designed by the architect Dennis Jones to be invisible behind the barbican wall as one approaches the Gatehouse. Thus it had to be partly sunk into the ground and the windows of the lower floor rooms look out at ground level onto the Garden. It was originally envisaged that these rooms would provide the conference facilities now afforded by the West Courtyard rooms, but in the event, after several changes of plan, they became further en-suite bedrooms.

Outside the walls of the Castle are various other residences for those who live 'in' College: several houses on the west side of Owengate, in the shadow of the Keep, house about 40 students; Moneyers Garth at the top of Owengate on its east side provides another handful of rooms; and the middle floor of Cosin's Hall was, in the 1990s, also converted into student accommodation (though it was relinquished in 2006 to the University's newly-established Institute of Advanced Studies). The biggest blocks by far, however, are Bailey Court and Moatside Court, together housing nearly 200 people.

The Castle's grounds are rather limited but, even so, are perhaps under-used. The Fellows' Garden has already been mentioned. Previously known as the Bishop's Garden, it became, in University times, the Dons' and then the Fellows' Garden – and as the last two names name imply, it was initially reserved by the College for the dons' use. That principle has, however, been gradually eroded to allow limited student access particularly during the Summer term. Plays and other events are occasionally staged there, and wedding photographs are taken there in good weather, but much more use could be made of what is a large and very attractive walled garden.

On the other side of the Barbican lies the Master's Garden, private to the Master except on a handful of social occasions throughout the year. Set in the Garden is the Master's House (an imposing seven-bedroom mansion on the corner of Owengate), acquired for the University by Bishop Van Mildert. It has been occupied by all Masters of University College except the first, Archdeacon Charles Thorp, who preferred a house in the College (i.e. the Cathedral Close).

Durham Castle in the early 18th century, by an unknown artist. Note the Coach and six – perhaps that of Bishop Crewe (1674–1721). The Bishop's (now Fellows') Garden is at the bottom left. The large square windows in the curtain wall (now blocked) provided light for a late medieval building against the south wall of the Courtyard, a building that appears to have been demolished in the late 18th century (since it is shown on a plan of 1775, but absent from Lambert's plan dated 1796); the redundant windows were probably blocked during Barrington's reconstruction and the building later replaced by the College washblock (unless that was east of the Gatehouse).

The Fellows' Garden building in the mid 1990s, with the Gatehouse and Keep behind.

The Fellows' Garden c.1900 (from an old postcard).

A path around the Castle mound leads behind the Master's House and onto the North Terrace. The Terrace is occasionally used by SCR members after formal meals in the summer – but it is, again, less than fully used. Two other areas have become sadly overgrown in recent years and cry out for care and attention: the Bishop's walk (once reputedly a skittles alley), to the west of the Fellows' Garden; and, a much larger area, the north mound (the glacis) of the Castle, which would make a wonderful terraced garden if funds allowed.

On a happier note, there is also the so-called Sun Parlour, the west slope of the Keep mound (mown, incidentally, like all the slopes with a Flymo on a long rope!). Here, as in the Fellows garden, the students exercise their privilege of access in the Summer term, and are even occasionally able to sunbathe as a rest from their revision labours....

This leads neatly onto a word about the roofs (for it is from the Sun Parlour that students frequently used to gain illicit access to the roofs). Some areas of the Castle (e.g. the Norman Gallery and Garden Stairs) have pitched slate roofs, while others have copper (the Kitchen) or lead (the Great Hall, Hall Stairs and the Tunstal Chapel) and the Black Stairs even has a small glazed dome. Thanks to a recent programme of repairs the vast majority of the roofs are now sound and attention can pass for a while to the ever-eroding stonework.

Lastly in this section, one should not forget an important outpost of the College, the Castle's boathouse, on the river-bank below the west end of the Cathedral, just up-stream of the weir, between Framwellgate and Prebends Bridges. This contains the eights and fours of the College Boat Club as well as two or three punts for more leisurely activity. There were once two covered Fives Courts in the Fellows Garden, though they have long since been absorbed into the back part of the Palace Green Library; and the lawn in the Fellows Garden is large enough to accommodate a tennis court for

A Garden Party in the Fellows' Garden following Convocation (Congregation) on 24/5 June 1889.

the dons' use; but this is, unfortunately, almost the full extent of the College's sporting facilities, for the Durham Colleges do not (in contrast with Oxbridge) have their own sports grounds.

[2] Durham Castle Museum

The University of Durham now boasts three Registered Museums, namely the Oriental Museum, the Old Fulling Mill Museum of Archaeology (on the riverbank next to University College's boathouse), and Durham Castle Museum.

The first two are easily defined in that they occupy dedicated buildings containing discrete collections, but the Castle Museum is rather different in that it shares its building, the Castle, with the living and working community that is University College, and also shares many of its artefacts as well. Thus many of the items classed as 'Museum objects' are in still in daily use and the boundaries between what constitutes part of the Museum's collection and what does not are often blurred.

All Registered Museums in this country now have a defined 'Collections Policy', and the Castle is no exception, being particularly interested in items relating to the Prince Bishops, to the Castle itself, and to the University (and particularly University College). Therefore, if an item has been in the Castle for a considerable length of time, or is significant to the history of the Castle, the College, or the Bishops, it qualifies for inclusion in the collections.

Much of the Museum's collection reflects the occupation of the Castle by the Prince Bishops, but there are also many artefacts and much archive material relating to the occupation of the building by the University. Thus we have collections of oil paintings, tapestries, arms and armour, silver tableware, crockery and some furniture, mostly of the late-17th and 18th centuries or later. Much of this material was collected by Bishops Cosin and Crewe between 1660 and 1721, but Bishop Maltby (1836–56) also left some of his furniture to the University and the University itself has also added its fair share of items.

A considerable proportion of the collection is accessible to visitors in this way, since large amounts of it are on permanent display around the Castle, though areas such as the State Rooms are reserved for other uses and are thus 'off-limits' to the Museum visitor except on special occasions and during specialist tours.

Income from guided tours was, at one time, 'ring-fenced' for the up-keep of the Castle: for a couple of decades after the restoration campaign of the 1920s and 1930s (for which see chapter 5.3), the money went into a 'Visitors to the Castle' fund, essentially a sinking fund for the maintenance of the building, until the University Treasurer of the time (Fitzgerald Lombard) deemed this no longer necessary. He presumably believed the fund was by then sufficient to meet future needs (he was sadly mistaken if so), and after that much of the income was given over for use on the historic contents of the Castle rather than on the Castle itself.

In 1962/3 the College's Governing Body accepted the invitation of the University Council to assume direct responsibility for College finances, after which the College's Bursar (Hugh Price, 1963–81, the first full-time Bursar) administered the fund. The Historic Buildings and Contents Sub-Committee (a sub-committee of the Governing Body) has since then suggested items of relevant expenditure. In recent years, however, finances have been centralised once more, and tour income goes into the central coffers for use on the Castle or elsewhere, as the University authorities see fit.

Under the current administrative set-up the Curator of Durham Castle Museum (the author, appointed in 1998) is a member of, and reports to, the College Council (as the Governing Body is now known), and the minutes of its meetings pass upwards from there to University Council, whose members technically make up the Trustees of the Museum. The Curator is allotted an annual budget by the University for use on the collections, and the Historic Buildings and Contents Committee (of which the Curator is the Secretary) meets three times a year, providing advice and expertise.

The Museum inventory (computerized since the appointment of an Hon. Recorder, the author, in the late 1980s) consists of nearly 1300 entries, but of very many more individual objects: e.g. DURUC (standing for Durham University College) item number 288 comprises 66 *oak kneeling stools* in the Tunstal Chapel, all upholstered with the arms of the see of Durham; and DURUC 965 comprises 24 *Victorian fiddle pattern table spoons* engraved with Bishop Cosin's fret. In addition to this, there are many items which are debatably part of the fabric of the Castle rather than Museum artefacts: obvious examples are the carved woodwork of the Black Stairs; and the Tunstal Chapel reredos, misericords and organ casing.

The Picture Collection

There are about 200 paintings in the Castle, of which a few are watercolours or engravings but the vast majority are oils. Most of these represent paintings from the collections of the Bishops (portraits of Bishops and royalty; representations of Durham Cathedral and Castle; more general landscapes) as well as paintings from the University era (portraits; further

Sir George Jeffreys (1644–89), by Sir Godfrey Kneller.

views of the Castle). Some are of considerable value in their own right, while others are of particular historical value because of their association with the Bishopric, the Castle and the University.

Examples of the former category include: an early copy of Hugo van der Goes' *The Descent from the Cross*, which can be seen today in the Tunstal Chapel; a very fine portrait of the 'Hanging Judge', Sir George Jeffreys; and J.W. Carmichael's 1847 image of *Durham Cathedral, Castle and environs*.

Durham Cathedral and Castle from Observatory Hill, by JW Carmichael, 1847.

Durham Castle: Fortress, Palace, College

Examples of the latter category also include the Carmichael as well as several oils and watercolours by Hastings, the best being entitled simply *Durham Castle*; Buckler's early 19th century watercolour of *The Courtyard, Durham Castle* and the ruined keep; and early 18th century oil and grizaille images of *Durham Cathedral and Castle*. Most of the images of the Cathedral and Castle within the collection now adorn the walls of the Black Staircase, though the Carmichael remains at present in the Senior Common Room.

Many of the landscapes and portraits were bequeathed to the University along with the building, i.e. they were part of the collection put together by successive bishops since the Restoration, that is Bishops Cosin (1660–72) and Crewe (1674–1721) and their 18th- and early 19th-century successors. Of the portraits some (but by no means all) are 'second copies' of bishops whose portraits can also be seen in the throne room of the Bishop's Palace at Bishop Auckland. One or two others (for example Judge Jeffreys) might have been left to us because they were no longer considered quite appropriate for a modern bishop's walls.

In recent years several portraits of bishops have been brought out from the State Rooms so that they can now be seen on the route of the guided tour: Bishops Chandler and Butler (during whose time the present State Rooms were being created within the shell of le Puiset's Hall) now grace the north wall of the Tunstal Gallery; while Crewe and Tunstal himself now hang in the latter's Chapel.

Durham Castle and Framwellgate Bridge *c.*1840, by Edmund Hastings (1781–1861).

Portrait of Bishop Nathaniel, Lord Crewe.

Durham Castle and Cathedral in the 18th century, by an unknown artist.

The Durham landscapes include some artistically poor but architecturally fascinating pictures of the Castle and Cathedral from *c*.1700 onwards. Now mostly hanging on the Black Stairs, they reveal all sorts of interesting details, such as the form of Hatfield's Keep before and after it became ruinous; and the presence of a balcony at the east end of the Great Hall in the 18th century. Similarly, two 19th-century interiors (both recently conserved and hung on the Black Stairs) show the Great Hall in transition: one (illustrated on page 44) shows the 18th-century panelling still *in situ* (*c*.1836), while the other (*c*.1850, reproduced overleaf) shows the walls stripped bare (prior to the installation of the present, later 19th-century, panelling).

Other pictures from the bishops' collection give something a 'snap shot' of the sort of thing one might expect to see on the walls of any 18th- or 19th-century country gentleman: there are a number of pleasant landscapes (of nowhere in particular); several small seascapes (one illustrated on page 112); a 'classical landscape' (in need of conservation and thus not on display); interiors (of, for example, a probably-imaginary Flemish cathedral); as well as a huge canvas of farmyard birds (formerly in the Senior Common Room but now temporarily relegated to storage); and the (still larger) White Peacock (on the east wall of the SCR).

enormous Foucault's Pendulum down the middle of the Black Stairs to demonstrate the rotation of the Earth.

The painter of Cundill was a County Durham man, Clement Burlison (1815–99), who was also responsible for a wonderfully-characterful portrait of Joe Bainbridge, Castle Postman in the mid-19th century (which can now be seen in the Octagon Room).

What was until recently the only other portrait of a Castle servant (hanging on the stairs to the SCR) is a sketch by W.A.Prowse (Vice-Master 1953–65) of Arthur Robinson, High Table Steward, whose career in the Castle spanned some 45 years from c.1932–1977.

The Great Hall looking north, c.1850, after the removal by the University of the 17th-century panelling; attributed to Edmund Hastings

With a few notable exceptions, paintings added to the collection during the life of the University have been portraits: the Great Hall houses portraits of many of the founding canons of the University, including Charles Thorp, the first Warden (hanging in pride of place behind the dais); and also (in the south-east corner of the Hall) John Cundill, the University's very first student (though he was painted only in later life). These portraits are not exactly exciting, but they do include some interesting characters, for example Temple Chevallier (high up on the north wall above the high table), first Professor of Mathematics and Astronomy, one of whose various experiments led him to hang an

'Calm Offshore'. One of a pair of seascapes by Abraham Storck (c.1635–after 1704).

The Black Stairs, from an early 20th-century postcard. The pendulum (removed by the early 1900s, the date of this picture), was actually a cannon-ball suspended from the skylight. The picture also shows panelling from the Cathedral's 17th-century organ screen, returned to the Cathedral in *c.*1966; and a full length statue, one of a series subsequently passed on to the Hancock Museum in Newcastle.

Arthur Robinson (1912–1995) by WA Prowse.

The Revd Temple Chevallier by CW Cope, RA (1811–1890).

113

John Atkin, by Andrew Ratcliffe.

The latest acquisitions are the portrait by Andrew Ratcliffe of Dr. Salthouse (Master 1979–98); a print of the Great North Gate, which straddled Saddler Street until demolished in c.1820, complementing a very different view of the same structure already in the collection; and, the latest addition to the 'servant's gallery', an oil painting, again by Andrew Ratcliffe, of John Atkin, MBE, supervising proceedings in the Great Hall as he has done for many years past.

Despite the size of the collection, there are still gaps worth filling: in particular, with the exception of two fine 19th-century views by Hastings and Carmichael, representations of Durham and its Castle dating from the University years are sadly lacking. This is perfectly understandable, since money has almost always been short and acquisitions other than portraits have almost always been by bequest or gift. In accordance with the Museum's Collections Policy, it is intended that this gap should be plugged (with prints if necessary) as and when funds allow, and that the Museum should continue to commission occasional new works.

Equally important, however, is the condition of the existing collections, and a steady programme of cleaning and conservation of landscapes and portraits has been underway for some time with the aim of restoring as many as possible to their full glory. In this respect the Museum already owes a debt of gratitude to the Fine Art Department of the University of Northumbria, whose M.A. students, guided by excellent tutors, have undertaken conservation of a number of paintings in recent years and have surface-cleaned many more. In addition, some more complicated conservation projects have been undertaken by graduates of the same department.

Examples of works recently restored are portraits of Charles II and his Queen, Catherine of Braganza (now visible in the Octagon Room); and two splendid landscapes of Jerusalem and Constantinople, now hanging in the SCR lobby.

The latter are just two of about 30 large canvasses and 22 coats of arms all recently brought back from the Bowes

Jerusalem, by an unknown late 17th-century artist. The picture is of some relevance to Durham Castle since Bishop Bek (1283–1311) was styled Patriarch of Jerusalem. (See page 44 for its companion-piece, Constantinople.)

Museum, the Durham County Museum in Barnard Castle, where they had been stored since 1949: a change in fashion had seen the removal of layers of paintings from the upper reaches of the Great Hall and the Senior Common Room and the subsequent storage of the surplus in the Bowes. These paintings were recently 'rediscovered' and retrieved, and their conservation has been the major item of Museum expenditure in the first years of the new millennium.

Some of these paintings have an interesting history: in particular there are two series of full-length depictions of Apostles, apparently acquired in Spain during the Peninsular Wars by the chaplain to one of the British naval fleets (though they are, unfortunately of much lesser quality and value than Auckland Palace's Zurbarans, acquired in a similar manner). One set (previously hung in the Common Room) belongs to the Castle's collections while the other series (which once hung in the Great Hall) is the property of the Cathedral Chapter and has been returned to them.

The Castle and Cathedral with the Bishop's Barge in the foreground, as found and at various stages during the conservation process.

The most important 'rediscovered' picture, however, is a view, painted sometime around 1700, depicting the Cathedral and Castle with the Bishop's 'state barge' on the river in the foreground. The 'new' picture has been restored with the aid of a generous donation by the Vice-Chancellor and now hangs alongside a similar view, painted from a different angle, which was already displayed outside the Bishop's Suite.

The College Silver

Some 300 catalogue entries relate to the College's collection of silver and electroplate, but that represents many more single items since many accession numbers relate to whole bundles of matching cutlery. The majority of the silver dates from the late-18th or 19th centuries, since it is what remains of the cutlery, table services and table candelabra of the early University. Very many items bear St. Cuthbert's Cross or other symbols of the bishopric and University College; and a number also bear inscriptions relating to the College and University.

The latter are not always the most valuable items, but are the most important to the Museum collection, since they have a definite historical link to the building. Important examples include the *Pemberton Bowl*, a George IV bowl given and engraved in memory of John Pemberton and now used as the centerpiece at High Table during Formal Dinner on a Thursday; a collection of George II and George III salt cellars, many inscribed with the initials of individual 19th-century undergraduates and presumably donated by the owners after graduation; and other items given by or in memory of members of the College.

There are also a considerable number of cups and shields relating to University sports societies, particularly the rowing club, a proportion of which are displayed in a dedicated display case in the Great Hall (since their earlier home, on a stand at the south end of the Hall is no longer deemed sufficiently secure).

The Pemberton Bowl.

Two handled cup given to the College in 1847 in memory of George Townshend Fox, MA.

Tapestries, Hatchments and Coats of Arms

Several sets of 17th-century Flemish tapestries adorn the walls of the Bishop's Suite, the Senate Room and the south wall of the Tunstal Gallery (and those from the north wall are in store). These once magnificent hangings are now somewhat faded and thus represent something of a restorer's nightmare, but they still add great character to the rooms concerned. The Senate Suite tapestries were in fact cleaned and partly restored in 1970/1 and the Bishop's Suite set and several other pieces in the early 1980s. Those in the Senate Suite depict various scenes from the life of Moses; while those in the Bishop's sitting room tell the story of Jacob.

The arms of Bishop Nathaniel, Lord Crewe, surmounted by a Bishop's mitre and a Baronet's coronet (since Crewe was also a Lord in his own right).

17th-century tapestry in the Senate Room, depicting Moses striking water from the rock.

Elaborate funeral hatchments were once hung outside the doors of the rich to announce a death. Those of Bishops Van Mildert and Talbot now hang in the Castle, the former over the fireplace in the Senior Common Room and the latter on the stairs to the Tunstal Chapel. Shields in stone, stained glass, and other materials can be seen all around the Castle, inside and out, showing the arms of various Bishops, while a great wooden Coat of Arms of Lord Crewe, once part of the 17th-century organ screen in the Cathedral, hangs over the fireplace in the Great Hall.

Wooden and other Furnishings

This is a wide-ranging category, comprising a large number of individual items, and here, perhaps more than anywhere else in the Castle's collections, there is some problem in deciding what should, and what should not, be categorized as a Museum object. For instance, how old, how interesting, and how valuable, does an armchair have to be before it should be classed as part of the Museum's collection?

It can be an important distinction to draw largely because it can directly affect the way in which an object is treated. For example, a damaged armchair might simply be disposed of by the College on the grounds that it was not worth repairing (normally a purely financial decision), but a Museum object is judged by other criteria and might therefore be set aside for restoration because of its importance in historical terms.

The largest kitchen table, perhaps dating back to the time of Bishop Fox (1494–1501).

A Gothic armchair, originally the Throne of Bishop van Mildert, now used by the Chancellor during Congregation ceremonies.

Examples that clearly qualify as Museum artefacts include items such as the antique muniment chests (displayed on the Tunstal Gallery); two 17th-century state arm chairs (also on the Tunstal Gallery); several antique oak settles; and a set of Queen Anne style dining chairs now in the Bishop's Suite.

Items where the distinction is less obvious might be the un-matched collection of armchairs in the SCR (they are not exactly distinguished pieces of furniture, but they are a traditional part of the furniture of the SCR); and the Great Hall dining chairs purchased in the 1970s to replace the long benches hitherto used by students in Hall. Most of the benches were disposed of, but one or two survive, presumably retained 'for the record', a pragmatic decision that might, or perhaps might not, be approved of by the Trustees of the modern Museum.

In a similar category to the benches are the huge wooden tables that once graced the Castle's Kitchen. Banished in the

1960s by Health and Safety regulations in favour of stainless steel worktops, the largest table now stands on the Norman Gallery and a smaller one outside the Norman Chapel (the remainder having been given to Raby Castle). These, however, undoubtedly qualify as Museum objects since they provide a fascinating insight into the working of the Castle in earlier times.

Marble, Plaster and Terracotta Busts

Included in the collections are about 10 busts, again typical of the sort of object that might viewed in a gentleman's house in the 18th or 19th centuries. Most are of marble but a couple are plaster casts and one is terracotta, all of them displayed on the Tunstal Gallery or the Black Stairs. Most interesting in terms of Durham's history are busts of several local worthies, for instance J.R.Fenwick (1761–1855), a local doctor, magistrate and Deputy Lieutenant of the County; but much the most valuable is a terracotta bust of George II by Rysbrack. Also displayed is a rare collection of 48 miniature plaster panels of *the Parthenon frieze*, by John Henning.

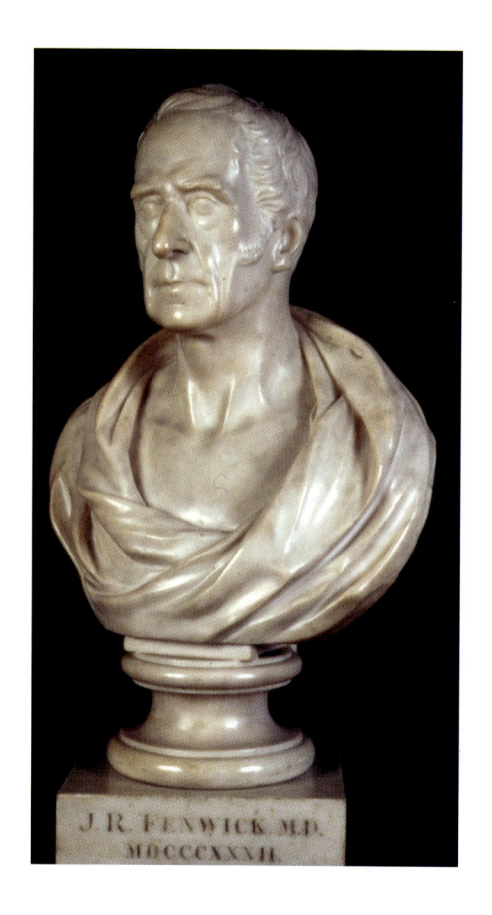

Arms and Armour

Some items in this category relate specifically to the militia of the County Palatine, the equipping and training of which was the responsibility of the Prince Bishops. The vast majority, however, is less obviously connected with Durham, having been transferred from Brancepeth Castle in and after 1922. Into the former category falls material displayed on the Tunstal Gallery, including five 17-century saddles and a drum bearing the arms of Lord Crewe. The Brancepeth material includes 28 sets of Cromwellian armour dating to the Civil War period as well as the equipment of a company

Drum bearing Lord Crewe's arms.

of a north-eastern regiment, the
Wallsend Volunteer Rifle Corps,
formed in 1803 – seventy sets of
Georgian Flintlock rifles, bayonets, powder horns, cartridge
cases and all the associated leather belts and straps. The rifles
and armour are displayed at the south end of the Great Hall,
above the Minstrels' Gallery.

Arms and Armour above the Minstrels' Gallery.

Stained Glass

Most of the stained glass is built directly into the windows of
the Great Hall and the Tunstal Chapel (and thus is perhaps
only debatably part of the Museum). There are also a few free-
standing pieces, the most remarkable
being a 16th century German panel
depicting the Judgment of Solomon.

The Judgement of Solomon.

China and Glassware

A College obviously contains very large amounts of china and glassware, but once again it is debatable how much of this belongs in a Museum. The most important item in the Museum category is undoubtedly the Maltby service, produced for the University at the expense of Bishop Maltby and already referred to above. The best surviving material is displayed on the Tunstal Gallery along with other items of tableware including, for example, a pint beer glass inscribed with the College Arms, perhaps the last survival of a once-common item.

19th/early 20th-century ewer and plate, just two of many items in the Museum's collection bearing St. Cuthbert's Cross.

Sporting trophies, previously displayed at the south end of the Great Hall, are now housed in a cabinet against the east wall.

Sporting and other memorabilia

As well as the sporting cups mentioned above, the collections include the oars won as a student by A.A. MacFarlane-Grieve (Master, 1939–53) and various other items, such as rowing and hockey caps, donated by *alumni* or their relatives. Some of these items are now displayed on the Norman Gallery.

Paper and photographic material

A considerable amount of paper and photographic archive material relating to the Castle is housed in the Palace Green library in the University Library's local collections, and more is held in the Castle itself. The archive includes records of all Castle students going back to well before 1950 (though unfortunately not right back to the College's foundation). Other items include early College concert programmes; many College photographs, formal and otherwise; as well as plans and photographic records of restoration work, and much more.

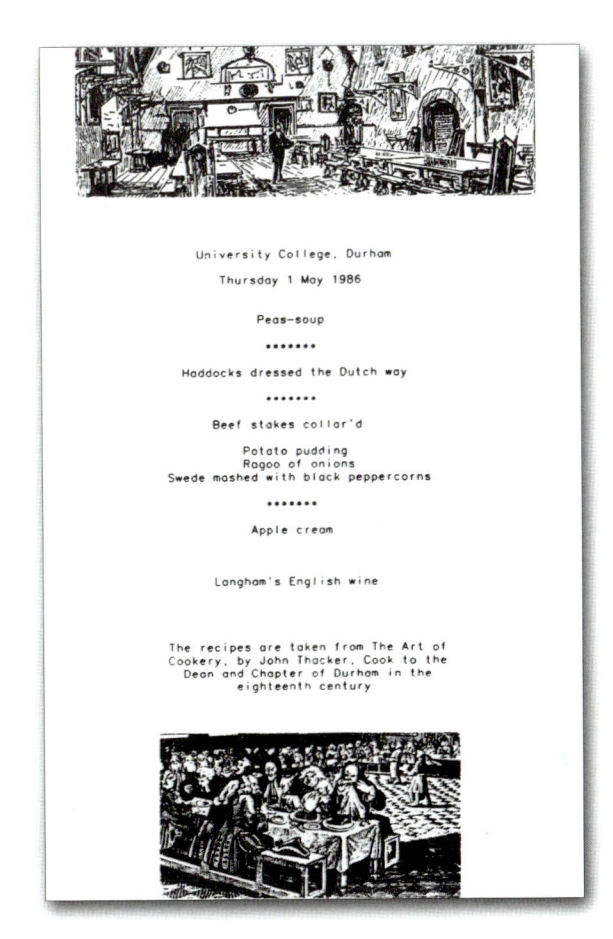

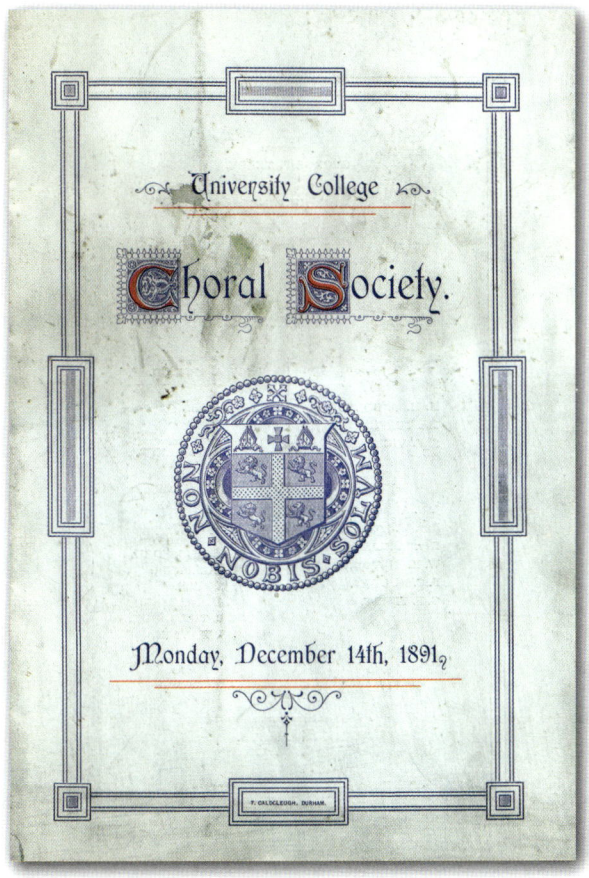

An illustrated menu from 1986 and concert programmes from 1923 and 1891.

[3] Caring for a Norman Castle: Fund-raising and Restoration

One of the on-going challenges for both the College and the University as a whole is the up-keep of Durham Castle. Partly because of the terms of the foundation, the University has never possessed sufficient funds to deal adequately with the day-to-day maintenance of the building. The inevitable result has been, for the last 170 years, consistent underspending on the fabric of the Castle leading to periodic crises when drastic action has become unavoidable.

This is, of course, a problem rooted firmly in the past: the Castle requires constant attention largely because it is built of soft, easily-eroded sandstone, and also because, unlike the Cathedral, the Castle's foundations rest not on firm bedrock but on layers of sandy clay, shale and broken freestone. Restoration work therefore began, of necessity, long before the University came into being, and some of this work has already been referred to above.

Most problematic was le Puiset's north range. Within fifty years of being built the seven-foot-thick walls of the 12th-century North Hall had begun to subside, and although the addition of the north-west tower in the early 13th century seems to have temporarily arrested the movement, its effects can still be seen today from Framwellgate Bridge and on the Norman Gallery itself.

By the mid-18th century the whole north range was again in danger of collapse as the north and south walls shifted apart, and the south wall of the Norman Gallery, which was by then bulging and overhanging, had to be cut back, re-faced, and tied to the opposite wall with wooden beams.

Substantial repairs had already been carried out on a number of other areas of the Castle by this time, including the strengthening by Bishop Cosin of the substantial buttresses to the Great Hall, but the topmost storeys of the Keep became so dangerous by the late 18th century that they were pulled down.

The danger to the North Hall was only temporarily averted for by 1900 it was once again in a very bad condition, and in 1904 large metal tie-rods were inserted in the structure to prevent further movement of the outer walls. Even so, within a couple of decades it was apparent that the north range and now also the west range as well were in a perilous condition: in 1927 a *Report on the condition of the Fabric* by the consulting engineer Oscar Faber stated that the Castle '*is in a highly precarious condition and any further delay in dealing with it may result in its total or partial collapse*'.

As a result the Durham Castle Preservation Fund launched a national appeal for funds in 1928, and the Castle's most major campaign of restoration in modern times (costing about £150,000, in today's terms about £4m) was undertaken between 1929 and 1939, with the majority of the financial resources being provided by the Harkness Foundation, an American-based charity now known as the Pilgrim Trust. The tie rods inserted in the north range had been intended to arrest the movement in the south wall by tying it to the relatively stable north wall. The result, however, had been the opposite: the south wall had continued to slump, but now began to drag the north wall along with it. Worse still, as the lateral walls resisted the movement, the south front bowed and major cracks appeared in the stonework. Faber's solution was to underpin the building with brick and concrete to reduce the pressure on the two walls and thus render them rather more stable.

The west range required equally drastic action, for the pressure of the building on the soft insubstantial bedrock had made the west wall of the Great Hall move outwards and downwards

The North west Tower from Framwellgate Bridge. Note the different vertical in the Norman and later windows (the large one at the top added by Bishop Hatfield (1345–81)), evidence of subsidence due to inadequate foundations.

Durham Castle in the 21st Century

Crack in the wall of the North Hall and the eroded stonework of Cosin's Porch, both in the 1920's.

Appeal posters, *c*.1929.

towards the River Wear. The steep hill made shoring impossible, so Faber's workmen had first to strengthen the walls by drilling holes through them and inserting large quantities of cement. After that large numbers of steel tie-rods were threaded through beneath the building to anchor both the western retaining wall and the west wall of the Hall itself to three huge blocks of concrete sunk deep into the Castle Courtyard. Finally, more concrete was pumped under the whole structure to anchor it to the solid rock beneath the loose stone. A large model, made as a record of the work on the west range, now stands on a landing of the Black Stairs, outside the Norman Gallery.

Even this, however, was not the full extent of the remedial work required at the time, for Oscar Faber, in a lecture in 1934, commented on damaged roofs, broken window heads *'and other matters too numerous to name, which, if unattended, will soon allow this noble structure to become a picturesque ruin'*.

The Times' reconstruction of the remedial works of the 1930s.

Boring in progress during the restoration work.

Tie-rods being inserted beneath the Great Hall in the 1930s.

Oscar Faber, CBE, consulting engineer.

Rt. Rev. H Hedley Henson, Bishop of Durham (1920–39).

Prof. Percy John Heawood, OBE, secretary of the fundraising committee.

In more recent times, Durham Castle has been the subject of various other rebuilding and restoration projects designed to maintain the historic structure. The restoration and rededication in 1951 of the Norman Chapel has already been mentioned. So too has the renovation of the Gatehouse in the early 1990s. The latter lay empty at the time (apart from the Porter's lodge) after the retirement of Cicely Shaw, the last resident porter, and a grant from English Heritage allowed the University to address the dual problems of dry rot in the roof space and badly eroded external stonework while converting the interior into student accommodation.

Numerous other smaller projects have also been necessary, some of them (such as the conversion of existing doors into sealable fire doors) modifications to the structure designed to comply with modern Health and Safety regulations. In addition, the first entirely new structure in 300 years was built in the 1990s: the Fellows' Garden building, designed by the architect Dennis Jones, provided much needed offices and student accommodation.

The most major project so far in the new millennium has been the repair and, in many cases, replacement of roofs. The weather is, of course, a constant threat. Water, in particular, slowly erodes the stonework and rots wooden structures underneath, thus eventually endangering the entire building and its contents. Over recent decades, the Castle roofs could not always be repaired adequately because of lack of funds.

Re-roofing of the Keep and Norman Gallery in progress, 2005/6, via a hoist behind Owengate.

Finally, in many areas of the Castle their condition became unacceptable, with water at times leaking into the students' bedrooms (on the Norman Gallery, on Hall Stairs, in the Keep, and elsewhere) and also on occasion anointing worshippers' heads in the Tunstal Chapel.

A major conservation project costing about £1 million was therefore undertaken between 2004 and 2006: the Northern Rock Foundation generously gave nearly £½ million towards the replacement of the roofs of the Norman Gallery, Junction and Keep ranges, which, with matching funding from the University, allowed most of the Castle's roofs to be refurbished. The work focused on re-roofing, but also included repair

Replacing the roof over the Tunstal Chapel (2005, top) and over Garden Stairs (2006, right).

Weather-damaged stonework on the North Range, 2005.

of associated stonework, the lightning conductors and asphalt walkways on the roofs.

The University can undoubtedly count this programme as a major success, but it cannot, however, rest on its laurels, for an ancient building such as Durham Castle requires constant maintenance. It is now the stonework that requires the most urgent attention, for the soft local stone erodes rapidly, and needs to be replaced regularly. Again, this is an area that has been neglected in recent years and a major campaign of replacement of worn-out stone is now overdue.

In addition, if the cycle of neglect followed by periodic crises is to be averted in the future, that campaign needs to be followed by a more concerted programme of day-to-day maintenance and repair of all aspects of the building than the University has hitherto been able or willing to undertake.

Stonemasonry is, of course, a particularly precious skill to maintain a structure like Durham Castle – but for many years the University did not number any stonemasons amongst its thousands of employees. It is pleasing, therefore, to be able to report that the University recently took an important step to ensure the long-term maintenance of the Castle with the setting up of an apprentice scheme for stonemasons, the intention being to build up a highly-qualified team to work on the stonework of the Castle. With financial aid from the Heritage Lottery Fund and the Learning and Skills Council, the University was able to initiate the scheme in 2004, apprentices being trained on behalf of the University by the masons of Durham Cathedral.

Fundraising for the maintenance of Durham Castle is, unfortunately, a constant problem. Although it is generally recognised that conser-vation is essential to maintain a World Heritage Site of this age and value, the Castle often misses out on the funding opportunities available to many other ancient monuments simply because it houses an educational institution. The government departments that fund education do not see it as their duty to maintain a Norman Castle (probably quite rightly), while those that fund ancient monuments do not see why they should fund an educational institution: thus virtually everyone agrees that the Castle is a worthy cause, but most people think somebody else should fund it! In other words, largely because the Castle is still in use as a 'living and working' institution, it is very hard to satisfy the criteria of the various funding and grant-giving bodies on which the University might call for help. At the same time, ironically, daily use of the building increases the need for conservation…

Time, weather, pests and daily use all take their toll on a building, particularly one as old as the Castle. Repair work, however, can only be undertaken at certain times of the year,

Eroded stonework on the roof of the North Range (2005) and inset, an apprentice stonemason at work.

partly because of the British weather but also because it must not unduly disturb the day-to-day life of the College or prevent enjoyment of the building by its many visitors. There are other constraints as well, for the Castle's dual role as both College and major tourist attraction enforces responsibilities of safety, access and security. Over the centuries theories and methods of heritage conservation have changed, and what was best practice 100 years ago might be considered unthinkable nowadays (legend has it that one fondly-remembered College handyman, Bill Grey, favoured the use of 6-inch nails for virtually all eventualities...). In addition, various materials such as asbestos, once in common use, are now considered unsuitable or even dangerous and, when encountered, must be removed.

Furthermore, various permissions must be sought before any substantial works are undertaken. In particular, Durham Castle's status as a Grade I Listed Building requires the University to seek Listed Building Consent for any changes which might in any way affect the fabric or the character of the buildings. Before the roofs were refurbished, for instance, English Nature rightly insisted that a bat survey was undertaken before any work started – though no current traces of bat activity were found. Archaeological monitoring has also to be arranged when any invasive work (such as the digging of a sewer trench) is undertaken, a service that is often delegated to members of the University's Archaeological Services (ASUD).

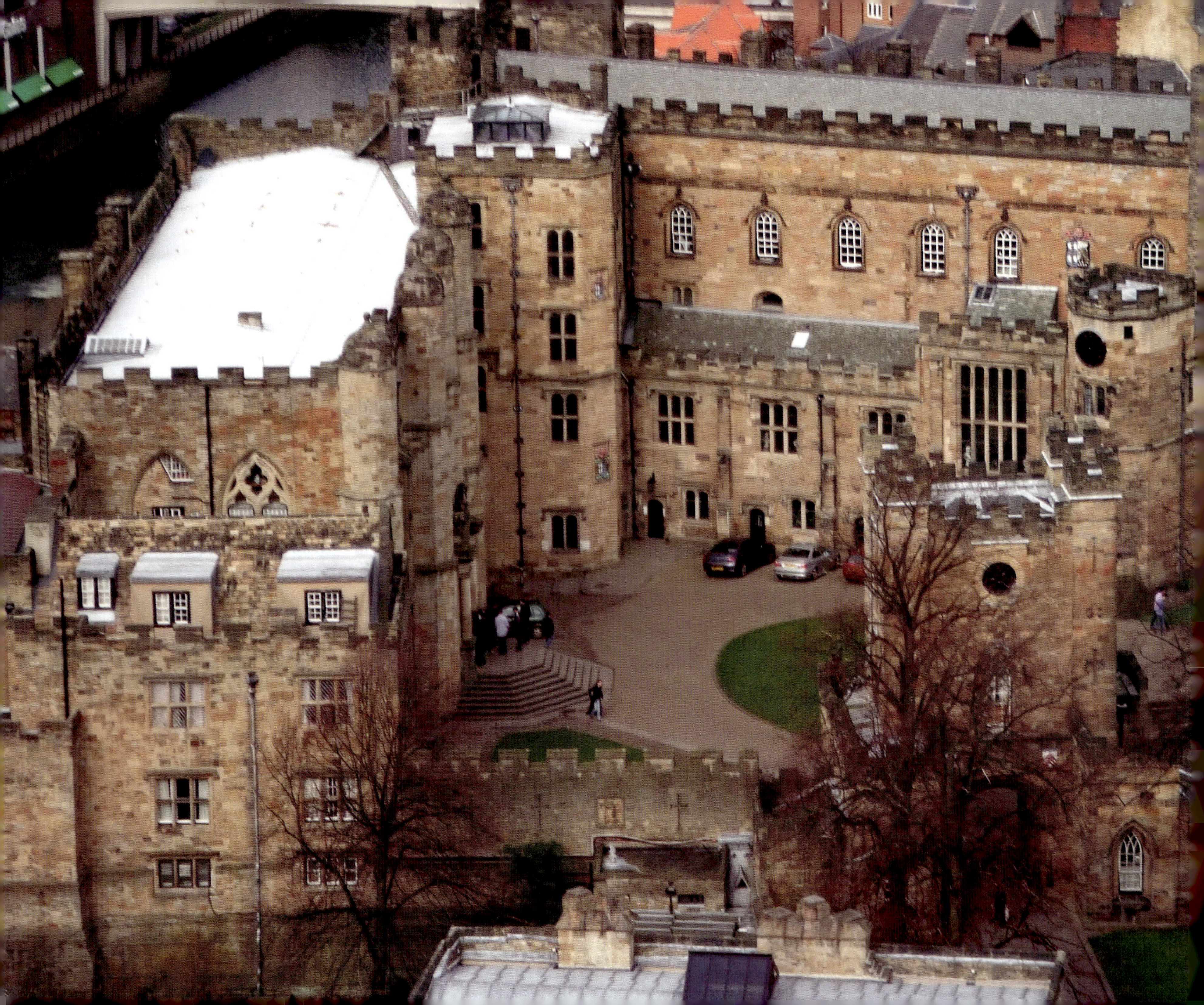

Chapter Six
The Way Ahead

[1] Durham Castle and Durham Castle Museum

The University celebrated its 175th Anniversary in 2007, with the Castle, the University's showcase building, playing a central role in the festivities. Meanwhile, an ambitious programme of renovation and improvements continues, aiming to return the Castle to a standard of repair and decoration that will allow it to become, and remain, one of the premier venues in the north of England for conferences, weddings and other prestigious events. This is, of course, not an end in itself: the real purpose is to raise sufficient funds to place the Castle on a secure financial footing, so that it can continue to be the centre of University College without becoming a financial millstone around the neck of the University.

As has already been highlighted, much of the soft sandstone from which the Castle is built is very decayed, and some is in urgent need of replacement. A limited amount of stonework was replaced during the re-roofing operations of 2004–06, but a great deal more needs to be done. In the long term, what the building requires is not periodic blitzes of restoration such as it has received in the past but a permanent rolling programme, such as the Cathedral already has, of repair and replacement of worn stonework – and with the setting up of the apprenticeship scheme the University is finally moving some way towards achieving this objective.

The Castle and Courtyard in 2007, complete with new roofs on the North Range and Garden Stairs.

Within the Castle Museum, much attention is currently concentrated on improving the displays on the line of the guided tour: this starts in the courtyard on the main steps up to the Great Hall; proceeds through the Screens Passage to the Buttery; passes through the Hall and along Tunstal's Gallery to his Chapel; doubles back along the Gallery to climb up the Black Stairs to the Norman Gallery; and finishes by descending the spiral staircase to the Norman Chapel and the Courtyard. There are, of course, other places of interest in the Castle, not least the State Rooms (the Senate Suite and the Senior Common Room) and the Bishop's Suite, but these are all in constant use for other purposes and so can only be included, by prior arrangement, in 'specialist' tours.

The Norman Gallery, together with the adjacent landing of the Black Stairs, is being developed as a useful temporary exhibition space with the addition of new display cases and the installation of five large chandeliers, the latter completely transforming the (often rather gloomy) Gallery.

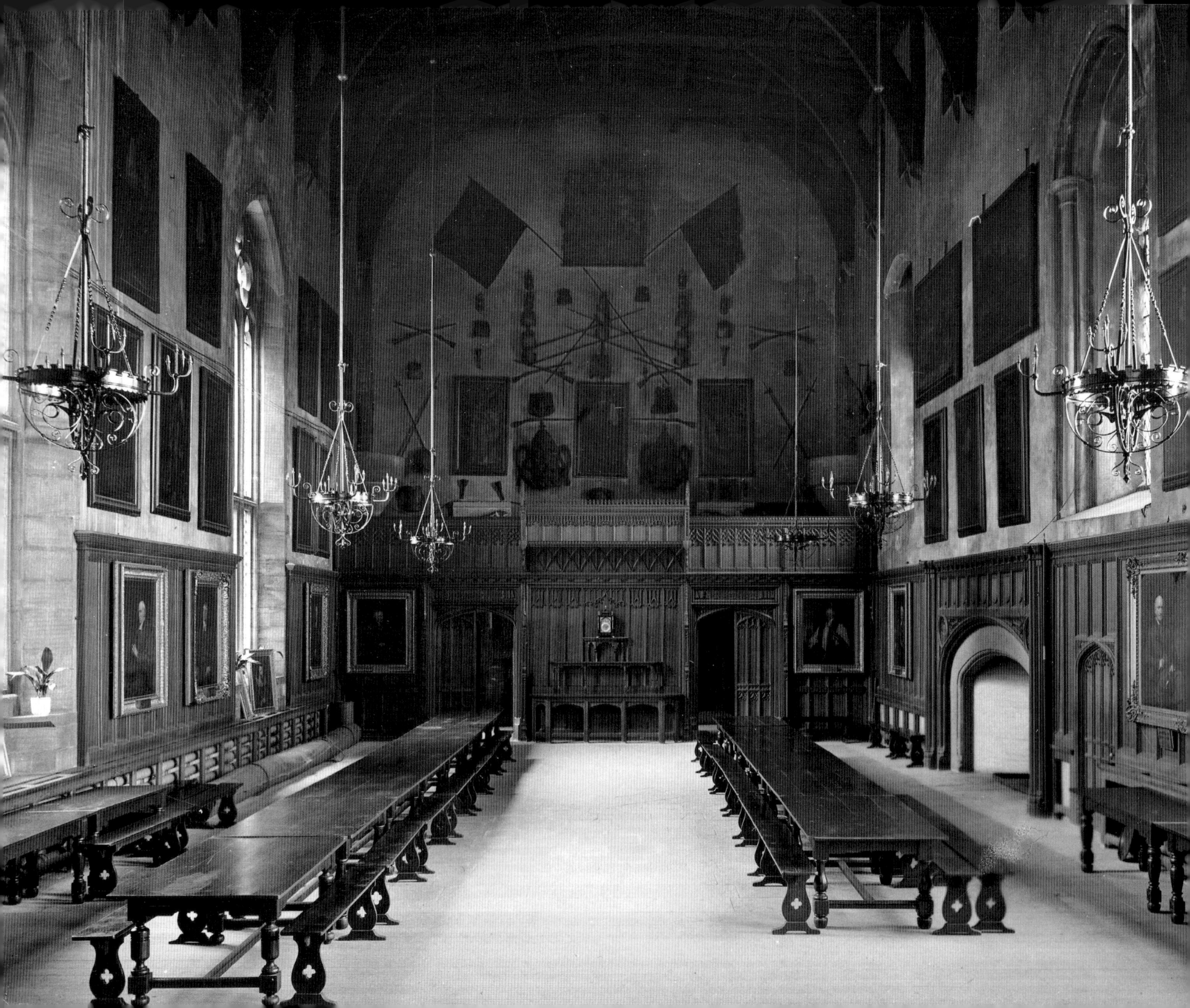

In the Great Hall, principal show-piece of the Castle, the decorative scheme is being reorganized to include additional layers of pictures and coats of arms. This will, in effect, restore the Hall to something similar to the décor of the late 19th and early 20th centuries – only less shabby then it then must have been! – and the end-result will be a quite magnificent banqueting hall, truly worthy of a World Heritage Site

Other plans to develop the Museum have, of course, to be tempered by the main function of the building, as the home of University College. One would like to make a visit to the Castle even more exciting, and it would be nice if it were a place where a tourist could spend a morning or even a whole day rather than just 45 minutes (the duration of the current tours, which are, incidentally, mostly student-led). Ideally one would like to do away with guided tours and allow visitors to wander at will, which is what the majority of visitors would prefer to do. However, this is not easily achieved while maintaining the security of the residents and the building, though we are looking at ways in which we might move towards that objective.

It would also be nice to increase the number and range of things that the visitor could see in and around the Castle. When I was taken to a castle as a small boy I was disappointed if I didn't get to climb the tower (preferably towers plural) to the roof; peer down (or drop things down!) the well; and crawl into the dungeons. We can't offer the latter (since the dungeons, such as they are, are buried with the remains of the Great North Gate under Saddler Street); but we could open up the well in the courtyard (though it might cause a bit of cursing from drivers of vehicles); and we ought at some stage to be able to contrive an safe vantage point on our newly-restored roofs from which visitors can view the Cathedral and the City.

The Great Hall: the early 20th-century decorative scheme.

To be truly viable as a 'Visitor Attraction' perhaps what is really required is a Visitors Centre providing educational and conference facilities as well as a shop and a tea room: these (particularly the shop and the tea room) have all become part and parcel of any modern heritage centre worth its salt, and the Castle suffers (financially and in other ways) so long as its lacks them. However, we are short of places to build or convert, even if we had the funds, so the idea must remain a 'pipe dream' for the foreseeable future.

[2] Durham Castle and University College

Currently the primary role of the Castle is, and is intended to remain, as a residential college of the University of Durham. University College is already, of course, an extremely popular and successful one, receiving more than ten times as many applications each year as there are undergraduate places on offer. There are, however, always areas open to improvement.

Durham Castle Gatehouse and the Cathedral from the Chapel roof.

A tour in progress in the Great Hall, 2006.

Along with all the other work on the buildings, the Castle continues to be adapted to make it ever more suitable for College life. Various recent improvements have already been mentioned – the refurbishment of the Gatehouse and Garden Stairs; the construction of a new office and accommodation building in the Fellows' Garden; the computer cabling of all student rooms; and so on – but the most eagerly awaited change so far as the students are concerned has been the refurbishment of the Moatside Court accommodation block in 2006. With no significant further expansion envisaged just at present, it seems unlikely that any major building works will be undertaken in the near future (there is, in any case, no obvious site for expansion available within easy reach of the Castle). In line with so many other organizations in this modern world, the College has a formal Strategy document, setting out the main aims for the next few years. In that document the primary objective of the College is outlined: 'to continue to contribute in providing that special Durham experience for the members of University College by maintaining a balanced, diverse, caring and inclusive community within which they can achieve academic excellence and acquire a range of life skills'.

Academic achievement is, of course, extremely important, perhaps ever more so in a world that seems to place increasing emphasis on paper qualifications – but there should also be room in a student's life for non-academic activities. There is little detail in the College's Strategy document of how the 'range of life skills' might actually be acquired, but perhaps it isn't needed: the College system by its very nature provides the opportunities; all the University has to do is to maintain it.

Within University College, 'Castle' as it is to every student past and present, the students and dons live, eat and socialize in close proximity. The College provides not only board and lodging but also many other aspects of life – dozens of clubs and societies, both sporting and otherwise, including the Chapel Choir, the College Orchestra and the Castle Theatre Company; regular Formal meals in the Great Hall; the June and Informal Balls and many other social events, many of them centred around the Castle Bar (the Undercroft, or the 'Undie' as it has been known for some time now); services in the Tunstal and Norman Chapels; the use of the College Library and Computer Rooms; and so on.

Thus, although students have to leave College to fulfil their academic commitments, most other requirements can be met within the College. This is not to suggest that students do not socialize University-wide – for, of course, they do. In a way, University College students have the best of both worlds: they are free to socialize in other colleges and elsewhere and to join

The Way Ahead

in the activities of the many University clubs and societies, but they also have, as the central plank of their University lives, their own College home in 'Castle'.

[3] Durham Castle: Hotel and Conference Centre

As well as housing the College and the Museum, the Castle now also acts during vacations as an hotel and conference centre. A major part of the College's income already comes from conferences, receptions, dinners and bed-and-breakfast guests, particularly during the summer months – and this trade looks set to continue and expand in the years ahead.

The Senate Suite, and particularly the main Senate Room, is in constant demand for dinners, receptions and as a conference venue, both in term and out. The Bishop's Suite, once reserved for the Bishop's personal use, is similarly in almost daily use, most frequently on a bed-and-breakfast basis. At present there are severe restrictions on who may be married in the Castle's Chapels (the privilege is confined essentially to current and recent Castlemen), but even so many wedding couples now choose to hold their reception in the Castle, either in the Great Hall or (if it is a slightly smaller gathering) in the Senate Suite (and the bridal couple normally stay overnight in the Bishop's Suite). We are booked up for wedding receptions on Summer weekends two or even three years in advance.

It is not all plain sailing, however. Modern hotel guests now expect en-suite rooms almost as a matter of course, but the Castle can offer very few such rooms (the Fellows Garden rooms and the recently-converted Garden Stairs rooms as well as the

The Castle and the River Wear from Bede landing.

staff, the office staff, and all the rest) feel and demonstrate tremendous loyalty to "their" College, and it seems that that feeling spreads outwards to infect all who come to live and work there – be they students, dons, or simply bed-and-breakfast guests.

[4] Durham Castle: World Heritage Site

Although the ancient portions of the Castle and their contents are now designated as a Registered Museum, the entire Castle is still very much in use and it is an excellent example of how successfully an ancient monument can be adapted to a new role as a modern university building. The Castle is, of course, with the Cathedral, designated a World Heritage Site, and the College is very privileged and proud to occupy such a building. It is worth repeating that within the University we are absolutely determined, despite occasional rumours to the contrary, to retain the Castle as a working residential college. We are also committed to widening public awareness of the building and to widening access to it in a manner that does not conflict with the academic life of the College. In short, we would like Durham Castle to be seen not just as the architectural centrepiece of the University of Durham but also as a focal point for the whole community.

The Great Hall set up for a function.

Bishop's and Chaplain's Suites being the major exceptions). Planning constraints, which quite rightly protect this magnificent building from wholesale change, mean that it is difficult and often impossible to up-date rooms to meet modern expectations, so this is an area where we cannot move so far or as fast as the more recently established colleges of the University. Nonetheless, many people enjoy the atmosphere and friendly welcome offered by the Castle, and bed-and-breakfast (and, to lesser extent, full-board) trade is flourishing and expanding.

The staff of University College (the Catering Manager, the Housekeeper, the porters, the cleaners, the kitchen

The Cathedral and Palace Green from the Castle Mound, Spring 2007.

The Courtyard in snow (photographed by EC Salthouse, Master 1979–98).

Appendix One

Prince Bishops of Durham

Walcher	1071–80	William Sever	1502–05
William of St. Calais	1080–96	Christopher Bainbridge	1507–08
Rannulph Flambard	1099–1128	Thomas Ruthall	1509–23
Geoffrey Rufus	1133–40	Thomas Wolsey	1523–29
William of St. Barbara	1143–52	Cuthbert Tunstal	1530–59
Hugh le Puiset	1153–95	James Pilkington	1561–76
Philip of Poitou	1197–1208	Richard Barnes	1577–87
Richard Marsh	1217–26	Matthew Hutton	1589–95
Richard Poore	1228–37	Tobias Matthew	1595–1606
Nicholas Farnham	1241–49	William James	1606–17
Walter Kirkham	1249–60	Richard Neile	1617–27
Robert Stichill	1261–74	George Monteigne	1628
Robert of Holy Island	1274–83	John Howson	1628–32
Anthony Bek	1283–1311	Thomas Morton	1632–59
Richard Kellaw	1311–16	John Cosin	1660–72
Lewis de Beaumont	1318–33	Nathaniel Lord Crewe	1674–1721
Richard of Bury	1333–45	William Talbot	1722–30
Thomas Hatfield	1345–81	Edward Chandler	1730–50
John Fordham	1382–88	Joseph Butler	1750–52
Walter Skirlaw	1388–1406	Richard Trevor	1752–71
Thomas Langley	1406–37	John Egerton	1771–87
Robert Neville	1438–57	Thomas Thurlow	1787–91
Laurence Booth	1457–76	The Hon. Shute Barrington	1791–1826
William Dudley	1476–83	William Van Mildert	1826–36, last Prince Bishop
John Shirwood	1485–94	Edward Maltby	1836–56, Bishop (only)
Richard Fox	1494–1501		

Appendix Two
University College Officers

Masters of University College

Charles Thorp	c.1839–October 1862
Joseph Waite	January 1865–June 1873
Herbert Edward Booth	July 1873–June 1874
Alfred Plummer	July 1874–June 1902
Henry Gee	July 1902–March, 1918
Henry Ellershaw	1919–1932
John Hall How	1932–1939
Angus Alexander Macfarlane-Grieve	1939–53
Leonard Slater	1953–1973
David W. MacDowall	1973–1979
Edward C Salthouse	1979–1998
Maurice E Tucker	1998–

Vice-Masters

Thomas Williamson Peile	1840–41
Charles William Whitley	1842–55
Robert Baldwin Hayward	1857–58
James John Hornby	1859–64
vacant	*1865–1917*
John Stapylton Grey Pemberton	March 1918–June 1919
vacant	*1919–39*
Edward George Pace	1940–47
Leonard Slater	1947–53
William Arthur Prowse	1953–65
vacant	*1965–70*
Stanley George Ramsay	1970–83
Duncan Bythell	1983–86
vacant	*1986–93*
Albert E. Cartmell	1993–97
vacant	*1997–2004*
Paula Stirling	2004–

Censors

Thomas Williamson Peile	1837–41
John Thomas	1837–42
Edward Massie	1842–45
David Melville	1843–45
Steuart Adolphus Pears	1848
William George Henderson	1848–50
George Butler	1849–51
Henry Harris	1852
James Gylby Lonsdale	1852–53
Philip Rudd	1853
James John Hornby	1854

Joseph Waite	1854–64
Edward Parry	1855–56
Henry Frederick Long	1862–64
Francis Frederick Walrond	1865–68
Frederick John Copeman	1865–78
Thomas Thornton	1869–77
James Atkinson,	1878–83
Walter Kercheval Hilton	1883–1913
William Douglas Lowe	1913–22
Angus Alexander Macfarlane-Grieve	1923–29
Alfred Guillaume	1929–30
Austin Pratt Whitaker,	1930–32
Claude Colleer Abbott	1932–41
Clifford Leech,	1941–46

Censor and Tutor in Arts

William Kenneth Severs	1946–49
Robert Thomson	1949–55

Censor and Tutor in Science

John Edwin Gregory	1946–53
Peter Christopher Jocelyn	1953–55

Senior Tutors

Robert Thomson	1955–6
Stanley George Ramsay	1963–83
Duncan Bythell	1983–90
John Ashworth	1990–98
Paula Stirling	1998–

Bursars

Luke Ripley	1837–40
John Thomas	1841–42
John Cundill	1843
William Greenwell	1844–47
William George Henderson	1848
John Pedder	1848–51
Philip Rudd	1852–53
Robert Healey Blakey	1854–58
Alfred James	1859–60
Henry Frederick Long	1862–64
Francis Frederick Walrond	1865–68
John Dixon Hepple	1869–70
Thomas Forster Dodd	1871–73
Thomas Thornton	1874–77
Walter Kercheval Hilton	1877–1913
William Douglas Lowe	1913–22
Angus Alexander Macfarlane-Grieve	1923–39
vacant	*1939–55*
William Scott Robertson	1955–57
vacant	*1957–58*
Stanley George Ramsay	1958–63
Hugh C. Price	1963–81
vacant	*1981–82*
Albert E. Cartmell	1982–97
Alan E. Gibson	1997–2004
vacant	*2004*
Shona Millar	2005–

Chaplains

John Cundil	1839–42
Thomas Garnet	1839–41
Brereton Edward Dwarris	1842–45
Henry Wade Hodgson	1843–46
William Greenwell	1846–47
George Edward Green	1848–49
Lewis Morgan	1847
Philip Rudd	1848–52
Godfrey Richard Ferris	1850–51
Joseph Waite	1852
Richard Chaffer	1853–54
James Raine	1854
Robert Healey Blakey	1855
Edward Parry	1855–56
Alfred James	1856–60
Charles John Robinson	1858
Henry Frederick Long	1862–64
Francis Frederick Walrond	1865–67
vacant	1868–75
Thomas Thornton	1876–78
James Atkinson	1875–83
Alfred Plummer	1877–96 (with intermissions)
Hastings Rashdall	1885–88
Beresford James Kidd	appointed 1888 but never came to Durham
Henry Ellershaw	1890–93
James Grove White Tuckey	1894–95
Dawson Walker	1896–97
Henry Alcock White	1897–98
George Harold Godwin	1899–1905
vacant	*1906–1911*
John Hall How	1911–12
Edward Pelham Pestle	1913–24
vacant	1925
Noel Dolben Coleman	1926–40

Chaplains of both University and Hatfield Colleges

Noel Dolben Coleman	1940–45
Ronald Claud Dudley Jasper	1946–48
John Charles Wallis	1948–57
Geoffrey Grenville Griffith	1957–66
Peter Graham Cecil Brett	1966–72
*Alan Hubert Nugent	1972–78

Chaplains

Philip Harold Emelyn Thomas	1978–83
Peter George Harold Hiscock	1983–87
Richard St John Jeremy Marsh	1987–92
Charles Yeats	1992–99
Benjamin Nicholas Gordon-Taylor	1999–2004
Anthony Bash	2005–06
Miranda Threlfall-Holmes	2006–

* last joint Chaplain of University and Hatfield Colleges. Subsequently the University College Chaplaincy was combined with the Solway Fellowship.

Curators of Durham Castle Museum

Richard John Brickstock	1998–

Appendix 3
A note on Sources

This book is based very largely on material from the Castle archives and/or the Durham University Library. Some of the most useful sources are given below.

Durham Castle

Durham Castle Guidebooks, of which the latest is
> D.Bythell, 1985
> *Durham Castle* (up–dated with additional material by M.Leyland, 1992)

W.Page, ed., 1928
Victoria County History: Durham, 3 volumes

M.Leyland, 1994
The Origins and Development of Durham Castle to AD 1217; the archaeological and architectural record, University of Durham unpublished PhD thesis

D.Rollason, M.Harvey, M.Prestwich, edd., 1994
Anglo–Norman Durham 1093–1193, which includes
> E.Cambridge
> *Early Romanesque Architecture in North–East England: A style and its patrons*, pp.141–60

M.Leyland
The Origins and Development of Durham Castle, pp.407–24

M.W.Thompson
The Place of Durham among Norman Episcopal Palaces and Castles, pp.425–36

M.Allen
The Durham Mint before Boldon Book, pp.381–98

C.E.Whiting, 1933
The Castle of Durham in the Middle Ages, Archaeologia Aeliana Series 4, Vol.10, 1933

M. Roberts, 2nd ed. 2003
Durham: 1000 years of history

N.Pevsner and E.Williamson, 2nd ed. 1983
Buildings of England: County Durham

D.A. Cross, 2002
The Paintings in Durham Castle, a catalogue, archive report

R.W.Billings, 1844
County of Durham, for plates of Durham Castle

University College

J.T. Fowler, 1904
Durham University, Earlier Foundations and Present Colleges, College Histories series

H. Gee, 1911
Durham Castle, 101–200 in R.S. Rait (ed.), *English Episcopal Palaces, Province of York*

C.E. Whiting, 1932
The University of Durham, 1832–1932 (which includes a list of authorities on the University)

E. Pace, 1937
University College and Hatfield College, pp.1–7 in C.E. Whiting, *The University of Durham 1937*

E. Jones, 1996
University College Durham, A Social History

Castellum, 1948–
The magazine of the Durham Castle Society, which includes

C.F. Turnbull, 1959/60
Student Life in the Castle, 1896–99

G.A. Williams, 1988/9
Pre–War Castle – The Thirties Remembered

K.T. Hoyle, 2004
Short Course No.4, October 1942–March 1943

A.A. Macfarlane-Grieve, 1922
A History of Durham Rowing

E. Bradley ('Cuthbert Bede'),
'*Ye Fresshemonne His Adventures at University College, Durham*' and other pictures and cartoons of life in Durham

R.E.H. Heady, 1995
Castlemen, Durham University Air Squadron and the RAF, 2 vols.

Index

Illustrations are given in italics

Abbey House, 79
Aldhun, Bishop, 13
Andrews, Thomas, 42
Archbishop of York, 22, 23
Atkin, John, MBE, 102, 114, *114*
Auckland Palace, 36, 38, *38*, 39, 52, 53, 110, 115
Aidan, St, 11, 13

Bailey Court, 4, 79, 80, *80*, 81, 86, 104
Bailey House, 79, 80
Bainbridge, Joe, *72*, 112
Balliol, King John, 22
Barbican, 29, 43, 91, 104
Barrington, Bishop Shute, 52, *52*, 91, 104, 140
de Beaumont, Bishop Lewis, 24, 140
Bede, Cuthbert, *3*, *4*, 58, *60*, 65, *65*, 66, 67, *68*, 98, 145
Bek, Bishop Anthony, 3, 22, 23, 24, 36, 44, 100, 140
Bell Tower, 32, 35, 65, *65*, 92, *93*
Bishop Hatfield's Hall, 24, 61, 64, 70, 100; *see also* Hatfield College
Bishop Middleham, 38
Bishop's Barge, *46*, 116
Bishop's Garden, *see* Fellows' Garden
Bishop's Hall, *see* Constable's Hall
Bishop's Suite, 21, 32, *50*, 51, 96, 97, *97*, 98, 117, 118, 119, 133, 137

Bishop's Walk, 106
Bishop's Wars, 41
Bishopton Castle, 38
Black Death, the, 29
Black Stairs, 3, *3*, 41, *42*, 43, 66, *66*, 93, 95, 96, 97, 98, 106, 108, 111, 112, *113*, 120, 127, 133
Boldon Book, the, 22, 23, 144
Bradley, Revd Edward, *see* Cuthbert Bede
Burlison, Clement, 62, *72*, 112
Butler, Bishop Joseph, 3, 48, *48*, 49, 73, 110, 140
Butler, the, 63, 72
Buttery, *30*, 31, 101, 102, *102*, 133,

Cambridge University, 57, 64, 70, 89
Carmichael, J.W., 108, *109*, 110, 114
Carver, Professor Martin, 13
Censor, the, 63, 75, 76, 77, 95, 141–2
Chandler, Bishop Edward, 48, 110, 140
Chaplain's Suite, 97–8, 138
Charles I, King, 41, 55
Charles II, King, 55, 114
Chester-le-Street, 4, 9, 10, 11, 13, 15
Chevallier, Revd Temple, 112, *113*
Clock Tower, 92, *92*
College Library, vii, 77, 100, 103, *103*, 136
Collingwood College, 84
Constable's Hall, 20, 24, 40, 49
Cope, Anna, 85

Cosin, Bishop John, 3, 42–5, *45*, 66, 73, 91, 92, 101, 107, 108, 110, 124, 140
Cosin's Hall, 4, 57, *61*, 63, 64, 79, 80, 104
Count Palatine, 21, 53; *see also* Prince Bishops
County Palatine, 21, 22, 120
Courtyard, the, 1, 2, 3, 16, 18, 19, 20, *26*, *33*, 35, 39, 43, *43*, 44, 46, *46*, 48, *53*, *54*, 72, *81*, *82*, 87, 91, 92, 93, 95, 98, 102, 103, *104*, 110, 127, *132*, 133, *139*
Crayke, 38
Crewe, Bishop Nathaniel Lord, 3, 42, 44, *45*, 46, 73, 95, 107, 110, *110*, 118, 120, *120*, 140
Cromwell, Oliver, 42, 55
Crow's Nest, 96
Cumin, Earl Robert, 14
Cumin, William, 19
Cundill, Revd John, 62, *62*, 73, 112, 142
Cuthbert, St, 9, 11, 13, 15, 117, 122

Darlington, 38
David I, King, 19
David II, King, 25
Dere Street, 9
Dissolution of the monasteries, 34, 55
Doyle, Dr Ian, x, 103
Duff, Sir James, 82
Dunholme (Durham), 11
Durham Castle Museum, ix, 5, 107–8, 133

Index

Durham Castle Preservation Fund, 124, *126*
Durham Castle Society, vii, 145
Durham Castlemans Society,
    see Durham Castle Society
Durham Cathedral, v, ix, 1, 4, 6, *6*, 7, *11*, 13, 15–16, 19, 21, 22, 25, 34, 39, 42, 44, *46*, 52, *55*–6, 58, *58*, 62, 63, 64, *65*, 71, 75, 91, 100, *101*, 106, 108, *109*, 110, 111, *111*, *113*, 115, *116*, 117, 118, 123, 130, 133, 135, *135*, 138, *138*
Durham Hall, Oxford, 55
Durham mint, 22, 144
Durham University, *see* University of Durham
Durham University Air Squadron, 78, 145
Durham University Journal, 16, 70, 76

Edward I, King, 22
Edward II, King, 24
Edward III, King, 25, 41
Edward VI, King, 35
Egerton, Bishop John, 48, 51, 52, 140
Elizabeth I, Queen, 35, 40
Elvet, 10, *11*, 19, 44
English Civil War, 3, 41, *55*, 120
English Heritage, 6, 128
Exchequer building, 29, 31, *31*, 41

Faber, Oscar, CBE, 124, 127, *128*
Fellows' Garden, 4, 66, 103, 104, *105*, 106, *106*, 128, 136
Fenwick, J.R., 120, *120*
Flambard, Bishop Rannulph, 2, 15, 16, 18, 19, 20, 25, 140
Fonteyn Doors, *100*, 101
Fowler, Dr J. T., *55*–6, 63, 64, 70, 145
Fox, Bishop Richard, 3, 31–2, *32*, 52, 73, 100, 101, 140
funeral hatchments, *49*, 118

Galilee Chapel, 19, 58
Garden Stairs, 19, 78, 101, 103, 106, 129, *132*, 136, 137

garderobes, 18, 39, *95*, 97
Gatehouse, *x*, 1, 18–19, 35, 52, *52*, 66, 86, 91, 92, 93, 104, *105*, 128, *135*, 136
Gee, Henry, 52, 141, 145
van der Goes, Hugo, 108
Great Hall, v, *viii*, 1, 2, 3, *5*, 6, 19, 23, *23*, 27, 31, 36, 41, 44, *44*, 52, 58, 62, 66, 69, 70, 73, *73*, 74, 75, 80, 82, *88*, *89*, 93, 96, 98, *99*, 100, 102, 103, 106, 111, 112, *112*, 114, 115, 117, 118, 119, 121, *122*, 124, *127*, 133, *134*, 135, 136, *136*, 137, *138*
Great North Gate, 1, 114, 135
Grey, Charles Grey, 69

Hall Stairs, *24*, 78, 92, 100, 103, 106, 129
Hardrada, Harald, 14
Harold II, King, 2, 14
Harrison Grimshaw, Geoffrey, 76, 77
Harrying of the North, the, 14
Hastings, Edmund, 44, 110, *110*, *112*, 114
Hatfield College, ix, 62, 78, 81, 82, 84, 85, 143, 145
Hatfield, Bishop Thomas, 3, 24, 25, 31, 32, 40, 58, 61, 73, 91, 100, 111, 140
Heawood, Prof Percy John, *128*
Henning, John, 120
Henry I, King, 19
Henry II, King, 35
Henson, Rt Revd H Hedley, *128*
Hodgson Fowler, C., 73

Inner Bailey, 1, 16, 19, 21, 23, 91, 104

James I and VI, King, 40, 41
James II, King, 41
James IV, King, 32
James V, King, 32, 40
James, Bishop William, 40, 140
Jeffreys, Sir George (Judge), 108, *108*, 110
Jenkinson, Dr John Banks, 56
Judges' Kitchen, 21, 98

Junior Common Room (JCR), vii, 84, 88, 92, 95, 96, 102
Jurisdiction of Liberties Act 1536, 34

Keep, *iv*, *viii*, 1, 3, 4, 16, 24, 25, *25*, 26, 27, 32, 40, 43, 44, 46, *46*, *54*, 58, *61*, 65, 69, 72, 73, 79, 81, *81*, 82, *82*, 91, 92, 93, 94, 95, 103, 104, *105*, 106, 110, 111, 124, 129, *129*
Kellaw, Bishop Richard, 24, 140
Kempe, C.E., 73, 75, 100
Kercheval Hilton, Walter, 75, 142
Kitchen, 3, 19, *30*, 31, 72, 101, *102*, 106, 119
Knocking In', 66, 67

Langley, Bishop Thomas, 29, 140
Laurence, Prior of Durham, 17, 19
Lindisfarne (Holy Island), 11
Lombard, Fitzgerald, 107
Lowe Library, 78, 103
Lowe, William Douglas, 76, *76*, 77, *77*, 78, 142
Lower Tunstal Gallery, 93, 94
Lumley Castle, 4, 79, *79*, *80*

MacFarlane-Grieve, Angus Alexander, 76, *76*, 78, *122*, 141, 142, 145
Maiden Castle, 9, 10, 11, *11*
Malcolm, King, 23
Maltby Service, 71, *71*, 122
Maltby, Bishop Edward, 58, *59*, 71, 107, 122, 140
Mary, Queen, 35
Mary, Queen of Scots, 40
Master's Garden, 43, 66, 104, 106
Master's House, 104, 106
Matilda, Empress, 19
Van Mildert, Bishop William, 4, 52, 53, 58, *59*, 62, 71, 104, 118, 140
Miller, Sanderson, x, 49
Minstrels' Gallery, 31, 103, 121, *121*
misericords, 37, *37*, 108
Moatside Court, *12*, 13, 80, *81*, 104, 136

Moneyers Garth, 31, 104
Morton, Bishop Thomas, 41, *41*, 140
Neile, Bishop Richard, 31, 41, 52, 140
Neville, Bishop Robert, 29, *31*, 140
Neville's Cross College, 79
Norham Castle, 11, 13, 16, 34, 38, *39*
Norman Arch, *2*, *3*, 20, 21, 93, 98
Norman Chapel, 1, 16, *17*, 18, *18*, 19, 82, *83*, 92, 93, 94, 120, 128, 133, 136
Norman Gallery, 3, *4*, *4*, 20, 21, *21*, 25, 46, 49, *49*, 51, 66, *66*, 92, 93, 94–6, *95*, *96*, *97*, 106, 120, 122, 124, 127, 129, *129*, 133
North Gate, *11*, 24, 28, 29, 40, 48, *48*
North Terrace, 43, *48*, 81, 106

Octagon Room, 51, *51*, 112, 114
Old Fulling Mill Museum of Archeology, the, 107
Oriental Museum, 107
Outer Bailey, 1, 15, 29, 48
Oxford University, 55, 57, 62, 64, 69, 70, 89

Pace, Edward, 62, 78, 145
Palace Green, v, 4, 6, *11*, 16, 31, 43, 57, 67, 80, 106, 122, *138*
Parson's Field Court, 79, 80, 81
Peohtwine, Bishop of Whithorn, 10
Pilgrimage of Grace, 34
Pilkington, Bishop James, 40, 140
Plummer, Alfred, 72, 74, 141, 143
of Poitou, Bishop Philip, 23, 140
Price, Hugh C., 107, 142
Prince Bishops, ix, 2, 46, *52*, 71, 107, 120, 140
Prince Palatine, 22, 29; *see also* Bishop Princes
Prowse, William Arthur, 112, *113*, 141
le Puiset (or Pudsey), Bishop Hugh, 2, 19, 20, 21, 22, 23, 24, 25, 32, 35, 36, 46, 48, 49, 51, 95, 97, 110, 123, 140

Ratcliffe, Andrew, 114, *114*
reredos, 73, 108
Restoration (of the monarchy), 3, 42, 55, 110

Rising of the North, 40
Robinson, Arthur, 112, *113*
Romans, the, 9–11, 13
Rufus, Bishop Geoffrey, 19, 31, 140
Ruthall, Bishop Thomas, 32, 35, 37, 140

Saddler Street, 1, *11*, 13, 28, 75, 80, 81, 114, 135
St Aidan's College, 84
of St Barbara, Bishop William, 19
de St Calais, Bishop William, 15, 18, 140
St Hild's College, 79
St Mary's College, 79, 84, 85
Salthouse, Dr Edward C., 114, *139*, 141
Salvin, Anthony, 57, 58, 91
Saxons, the, 10–11
Screens Passage, 31, 100–1, *100*, 133
Senate Suite, 40, 41, 51, 93, 94, 98, 118, 133, 137
Senior Common Room (SCR), 5, 20, 21, 32, 49, 73, 84, 85, 88, 97, 98, 100, 110, 111, 112, 114, 115, 118, 119, 133
Servery, 84, 100, 101
Shaw, Cicely, 86, 128
Smith, Dr Samuel, 62
stained glass, 73, *73*, 75, 100, 118, 121, *121*
State Rooms, 5, 45, 49, 52, 97, 107, 110, 133
Stephen, King, 19, 22
Sunderland, 1, 15

The Adventures of Mr Verdant Green, 68
Thorp, Archdeacon Charles, 56, *56*, 57, 60, 62, 64, 65, 71, 73, 92, 95, 104, 112, 141
Thurlow, Bishop Thomas, 46, 140
Trevor, Bishop Richard, 3, 48, *49*, 51, 140
Tunstal (or Tunstall), Bishop Cuthbert, 3, 23, 34, 35, *35*, 36, 39, 40, 41, 44, 51, 73, 91, 92, 140
Tunstal Chapel (also Tunstal's Chapel), vii, *34*, 41, 44, 58, 73, 75, 77, *77*, 92, 93, *93*, 94, 106, 108, 118, 121, 129, *129*, 133

Tunstal Gallery (also Tunstal's Gallery), 3, *3*, 51, 66, 71, 75, 93, 94, 98, 110, 118, 119, 120, 122, 133
Turnbull, C.F., 75, 145

Uchtred, Earl of Northumbria, 10, 13, 17
Undercroft, 1, 3, 16, 24, 70, 82, *82*, 84, 92, 102, 136
University College, vii, ix, x, 4, 13, 55–90, 102, 103, 104, 107, 108, 117, 133, 135–7, 138, 141–3, 145
University College Boat Club, 66, 67, 77, 106
University College Choral Society, 70, 73
University College Durham Trust, vii, x, 102–3
University House, *see* Cosin's Hall
University of Durham, v, ix, x, 55–90, 4, 53, 88, 107, 135, 144, 145
Unversity College Arms, 61, 122
Ustinov, Sir Peter, *89*

Walcher, Bishop of Durham, 1, 15, 16, 18, 19, 140
Waltheof, Earl of Northumbria, 1, 15
Water Gate, 1
Wear, River, v, 1, 9, 10, 11, 15, 44, 46, 63, 79, 117, 127
Wearmouth, 1, 15
Wesley, John, 52
West Courtyard Room, 102, 104
West Courtyard, vii, 102, 104
White, Revd Henry Alcock, 75, 143
Whiting, C.E., 29, 62, 70, 78, 144, 145
William IV, King, 57
William Rufus, King, 15
William (the Conqueror), King, 1, 14, 15
Wolsingham, 38
Wyatt, James, 52, 91, 92

Ye Fresshemonne His Adventures at University College, Durham, 60, 66, 68